MW01595103

From Glory to Glory

Achieving Holiness in the Season of Singleness and Marriage

Robin Webster, MS, LPC, NCC

Divine Writer's Publishing, LLC

Blessings upon your future!

Robin Webster MS, LPC, NCC

Celebrating From Glory to Glory

"The title and theme of this book is prophetic and timely for this age. The message is also personified in its author. I have watched Robin Webster live these principles in real time and in real life. Everyone should read From Glory to Glory: Achieving Holiness in the Season of Singleness and Marriage. It is a game changer."

- BISHOP RC BLAKES, JR., NEW HOME MINISTRIES

Dedication

This book is dedicated to my mom and late father as well as my beloved future husband. To my parents, I'm so thankful for God's gift of life to me through you. You've nurtured me, protected me, affirmed me, loved me beyond words and introduced me to the overflowing well of life that comes with accepting Christ. Thank you for showing me what a godly marriage looks like so that I may walk in the fruit of it and pass this reflection of Christ's love for the church to the fruit (children) of my womb.

To my love, my future husband, my tailor-made man of God, God already knows you and He has built us suitable for one another. He knows the perfect time for our meeting. Throughout my life I have been mindful of your existence and my position at your side. Thank you in advance for covering me, for further nurturing me, for setting a platform for me to further evolve "with" you and for protecting my heart as I do the same unto you. When I say, "I do," I'll mean it and my continuous actions towards you will confirm it. Cheers to our forever as God will get the glory from our love story.

Copyright © 2022 Robin Webster, MS, LPC, NCC

All rights reserved. No portion of this book may be reproduced, stored, in a retrieval system, or transmitted in any form or by any means- electronic, mechanical, photocopy, recording, scanning, or other – except for brief quotations in critical reviews or articles, without the prior written permission of the author and publisher. For permission requests, write to the publisher, addressed, "Attention: Permissions," to the email below. Published in Gretna, LA by Divine Writers Publishing.

Books may be purchased in bulk for educational, business, fund-raising, or sales promotional use. For more information, please e-mail lareinalegad083@gmail.com or call 504-407-1673.

Unless otherwise noted, scriptures taken from the New Living Translation, King James Version, New King James Version®. Copyright © 1982 by Thomas Nelson. Used by permission. All rights reserved.

Library of Congress has cataloged this edition as follows:

Library of Congress Control Number: 2022905981

ISBN Hardback 979-8-9859252-0-3
ISBN Paperback: 979-8-9859252-1-0
ISBN eBook: 979-8-9859252-2-7

Printed in the United States of America

Contents

Introduction

As I began this manuscript, God prompted my spirit to write a book. Even so, the demands of life and not knowing exactly what to write about is what held me back. As a 38-year-old woman who has been a counselor for the past 15 years, five of which I have been a Christian Counselor in private practice, there is so much that I've heard, interceded for, and even experienced personally that I found myself stuck not knowing where to begin. With the topic not yet fully revealed the only thing I knew was that I wanted to uplift and enlighten my readers. Then, it finally hit me... or should I say, the Holy Spirit revealed it to me.

I'm very passionate and have always been so about healthy, thriving marriages and relationships. I've always enjoyed helping others achieve optimum health in their relationship with self and others. Through God's grace, I've been successful at it for many years. Since the health, healing and restoration of others is what God has called me to on Earth to help facilitate, I am especially filled with joy when I see a relationship that was once broken now fortified and reconciled. Each day I get the opportunity to experience God using me as a vessel to pour His healing on what He ordains. I'm equally excited and blessed as I witness the intentional work and investment of those I see in and out of therapy remain committed to executing their part in the success of their relationships, including their relationship with themselves.

Regarding my personal life, specifically romantic relationships, I have prayed since I was a little girl for my husband. I prayed for his protection and our future marriage (I am currently single) long before I really understood the concept of marriage. I did this because my mom encouraged me to. My mother would literally say, "Repeat after me, "Dear God, please bless my husband and keep him safe, etc.," until her guidance was no longer needed for me to cover him in prayer. Because I have not yet met my life partner in the form of my husband, I now understand my mother's logic as her teachings were used by God to prepare me for my life calling and journey on my route to covenant matrimony, which is a journey that is still in progress.

Even so, my personal understanding of marriage and healthy relationships comes not only from prayer but also from learning how to be married to Christ first. I've learned that the season of singleness is a season of training where great wisdom is gained as we stay in the face of God, seeking His counsel, adhering to His percepts and embarking on the journey of self-discovery uninterrupted. I encourage others in the season of singleness to not rush into marriage. The point that I'm making is that if our relationship with self and God as a single is underdeveloped, immaturity is what our marriage will be forced to contend with if we rush this stage and marry out of season. Please believe me when I say that marriage is a godly institution for the mature in spirit and not for the faint at heart.

A Kingdom marriage that thrives is based upon a firm foundation of maturity in God as it represents Christ's love for

the church. As I go deeper with this statement, my question to both the single (unmarried) and the married (in holy covenant) is this, "Are you equipped for trouble?" That is, when trouble in your marriage strikes, do you know that you have the fundamentals to slay the forces of darkness that will inevitably try to come against your marriage?

When I state the fundamentals I'm speaking of the spiritual strength through prayer and God's word, the knowledge of how to cover and communicate with one another effectively, the wherewithal that when you go through a moment or season of long suffering in your marriage that you have cultivated a solid relationship with God so much "out" of the storm that it is equipped to cover you and your love while "in" it.

Am I saying that you should be an "expert" in all of these things before proceeding in marriage? No, but what I am saying is that you "should" have enough of this information in your toolbox when going into marriage to give yourself a good head start and build upon it along the way.

In 1 Corinthians 7:28, the Apostle Paul warns us that it is better for us to remain single because when we decide to get married, we will certainly have trouble. He did not make this statement to say that marriage is bad because it is not, however he did make this statement for us to understand that in marriage, we are signing up to have trouble due to the things that it will entail. I can go further to state that because marriage represents Christ's love for the church, it is most certain that the devil in hell is going to try to destroy anything that stands to represent and re-present Christ's love for it. This statement is not intended to scare anyone from marriage, but it is shared to give insight to the fact that marriage is serious business.

This is why it is intended for the spiritually mature because of some things that a married couple will have to face to remain steadfast in their union. This is not to say that there will not be lovely moments and experiences in marriage, but it's important to know that marriage is work. You must maintain it by constantly investing in God and in each other together as you attend to each other's ever evolving needs. I also feel that it's important to stress that when investing in your marriage, please do not take on the task of doing this without the input of God or without drawing from His strength. So many take on the stance of having to perform and do the work of investing in their marriage without involving God's insight. When we do not involve God in this endeavor (as with any other) this eventually causes unnecessary burnout and puts unwarranted stress on the marriage.

If marriage is ever to be a fairytale and to be thoroughly enjoyed, it will only be achieved through spiritual maturity, prayer, meditating on God's word, constant communication and transparency, friendship, love, sexual and emotional intimacy, respect, fun, safety in vulnerability, seeking wise godly counsel when needed and dying to self (one's own selfish wants and needs) for the greater good of the other and so much more. These consistent actions, among others, yield beautiful results that require intentionality and great investments made throughout the union.

Marriage is engineered to make us look like Christ and His love for the church, giving of Himself for it. This is the reason why spiritual maturity in marriage is a must and why having peace along with confirmation from God is imperative before saying, "I do."

When things get tough in your marriage and you have to roll up your sleeves to address things of great weight, it's your confirmation from God along with the peace that you received from God to move forward in becoming one that will serve as your umbrella of grace that will help you to stay committed. It's this grace fueled by God's confirmation that will support and guide you. Since God called and confirmed you to walk with your beloved, you will both overcome your issue together with divorce not being a contemplated or selected solution to your temporary issue. After all, a threefold cord is not easily broken (Ecclesiastes 4:12).

Waiting Well

During my wait in the season of singleness, I have truly learned that if I can be faithful to that in which I cannot see (God), then I am surely able to be faithful to that in which I can (my earthly husband). I have had the opportunity to learn to operate in the fruits of the Spirit in which God gives us all crash courses in - love, joy, peace, patience, kindness, goodness, faithfulness, gentleness and self-control.

As a teen, I asked God and gave Him permission to use my life for His glory. With asking and giving God the permission to do this, I had no idea that the areas that He would capitalize on was my singleness and the area of my love life. I joke with my friends all the time about how God is trying to get all of the oil, seeds, rinds, pulp, and everything that there is to be gotten out of me on this waiting journey, especially because God has answered my prayers in virtually every other area. This process of waiting has caused me to tap into exercising the fruit of the spirit.

- "Patience" with God's timing in presenting me to my husband

- "Self-control" when it comes to my actions with delaying sexual gratification

- "Faithfulness" to God's word because it takes trust and surrender to accept God's "no" in a microwave world and still remain hopeful

-"Goodness" because even when I must face unideal circumstances whether in my health, business or things going on around me, I must still hold on to the good news and truth of God's word as I navigate the remedy with His leading

- "Kindness" has had to be exercised because of having human moments when I just want my way, can't have it yet, I still must show up and interact with God and others with a pure surrendered heart. This means that while acknowledging to God what I feel, I cannot allow my feelings to negatively affect my actions towards others and must still be kind.

- With operating in the fruit of the spirit of "joy," even while not always having things go my way, the joy of the Lord is my strength which causes me to still have a joyful outlook

- The fruit of "peace" within me is applied because I do not forfeit even when I see nothing changing in my circumstance. When it comes to my "peace," relinquishing it is non-negotiable because along with God, it is what fuels my strength and my ability to operate in my giftings.

My process has not always been the easiest; however, I know that God knows what He is doing. Since He is not practicing when it comes to the details of my life which includes my love life, I know that this purification process solicits me to walk in the fruits of the spirit only to make me more equipped to receive and accommodate what I've prayed for in every area that I'm believing God to bless me. The fruits of the spirit are needed in marriage, parenting, running a business and every relationship that involves us interacting with people.

As a firm believer of learning the lesson so that I do not have to repeat the course, I've learned how to call upon the Lord by being reliant on Him as my sustainer and not put that pressure on another person by experiencing the weight of what that feels like when it was once done to me. When my father died, God showed me that if I chose to put men in His place to fill my void, I would only discover through the unrelenting pain of disappointment that only He could fill the need of my father's love, comfort and affirmation, not men. This is what has caused me to practice seeking God as my "first" support opposed to my secondary because He is the only one that can handle the brunt of the spiritual weight that comes with some of life's events, and I should never put the totality of that weight on a human being to relieve me of.

Because I understand this, I know that putting the bulk of the weight on God and seeing my husband as a secondary support is another way that I keep God first and honor Him as Sovereign. In addition, this is what will allow my husband to be human and maintain the role *after* God as my support and covering which is realistic.

Waiting has allowed me to accept the woman that I am by embracing my power and learning how to operate in my life's purpose. This has been done by recognizing my God given gift and strength as a healer, motivator, well of wisdom and a safe place for people to be supported in evolving. Additionally, I acknowledge my power as a giver of love and as one who encourages. This calls forth the greatness in others, disciples them, and encourages me to strive to live as an example of holiness and humility.

I could not have gained the understanding of my strength and call without opposition from society and even love interests in the past. The opposition or lack of support caused me to dig deeper into believing what God revealed to me about me. It can be further mentioned that knowing my life purpose and calling will illuminate my partner in purpose. I will explain this as we go along. It can also be mentioned that I've learned how to hear the voice of God because in many instances, it *has* just been He and I.

To hear the voice of God, you must be knowledgeable of His word through reading the Bible because the things that He will say, (no matter the topic), will line up with His word. For example, I was dating a man that I really liked and one day in the middle of taking a "good nap" (you know, the nap that is so good that when you wake up the same day it feels like a new day), I began to stir, and his face appeared in my mind. Immediately after stirring and seeing his face appear in my mind, a voice that I knew was God stated, "He's not the one." Upon hearing this, I woke up, tried to dismiss it and told myself that, "I must be trippin!"

Because I'm familiar with the voice of God and how the Holy Spirit leads, after having a mini tantrum in my bed I said, "God, then why did you let me start liking him?!!" After that I dismissed it from my mind but said that I would just have to see how it played out. After about a week, my love interest and I had a conversation about his health which was actually a follow up conversation since he expressed to have health issues that he acknowledged to not be taking seriously.

Since I had experienced the pain of losing my father and my love interest at that time had a 15-year-old daughter, I further encouraged him to address that particular health concern and take precautionary exams due to him being in his forties and because I wanted his daughter to have him around for as long as possible. Even so, it was in that last conversation that it was confirmed that what I was told by God in the middle of my nap was true. Since my love interest and I were dating with purpose and we were doing so in pursuit of marriage, when he expressed to me that he was "not" going to address the issues, I immediately remembered Ephesians 5:28-29 where it states, "In the same way, husbands ought to love their wives as they love their own bodies. For a man who loves his wife actually shows love for himself. No one hates his own body but feeds and cares for it." Now, although we were not married, we were getting to know each other and dating with the purpose to see if there was a possibility for marriage.

Because he expressed his intent to be my covering (husband), his disregard for managing his own health confirmed that what God was telling me about him not being the one for me was true. After we went our separate ways and a few months passed, the guy informed me that he later became diagnosed with cancer and because I was encouraging him to get things checked out while we were together, despite his initial reluctance, he knew that God was trying to save his life by using me to get his attention. This further taught me that sometimes God allows us to be connected to people in close up positions in order for Him to speak to them through us.

Needless to say, but I feel the need to say, not all connections between male and female are meant to be romantic. Sometimes we connect in a relationship for God to relay a message. You will know the meaning for your relational connection as you grow in God. This is done by reading the Bible to hear and know His voice (Holy Spirit) because God only speaks what He said which is located in the Holy Bible. If it does not line up with what is in the Bible, then God did not say it. In my situation, God was simply telling me that my love interest was "not the one" that I was to marry because my position with this man was to help in the process of saving his life. During this time of my waiting, God has also given me the ability to feed my spirit in such a way that my flesh does not dictate my decisions. (For this, I give God the praise as I can take no credit for this God given anointing.)

My parent's marriage taught me about the characteristics of holy matrimony. With witnessing their union, I learned that a Christ centered marriage exemplified cohesiveness, godliness, peace, support, love, selflessness, respect, fidelity, self-control and commitment until death do you part. Watching my parents walk out their vows throughout my life has blessed me immensely, but of all of the things that their marriage taught me, the paramount thing that I took away from them was their commitment to God and each other.

Seeing my mother at my father's bedside as he began to

transition to be with our Lord was the hardest, yet most power-ful thing that I have EVER witnessed in my life. Even as I write this, I get emotional because it was a powerful testimony and reflection of Christ's love for the church. My mother remained FAITHFUL to God's word and her word in love and in deed like the pain of the cross which Christ carried before and with her through this process.

I've always prayed and asked for godly discernment and wisdom as my father instructed me from childhood. Because of that, I discovered my life's calling at the age of 15. To cover all bases - natural and spiritual, I majored in psychology during undergraduate studies and went onto graduate school. I studied Professional Community Counseling with a focus in Marriage and Family Therapy, became nationally certified to counsel and went further to become a licensed professional counselor.

Because of the knowledge that I have of how to have healthy relationships, there have been times when I questioned the reason why God allowed me to have this wealth of wisdom and knowledge, place me in position to teach others, and witness their marriages and relationships restored, yet still render me absent of having my own fruit bearing union. After much thought and prayer, the answer to this question is that God's perfect timing for my husband and I to connect has not yet come, and our platform of becoming one is still in the state of being fortified.

It truly took much prayer and faith to arrive at this understanding and with this being revealed to me, the Lord placed Proverbs 10:22 in my spirit. "The blessing of the Lord makes one rich, and He adds no sorrow with it." With the truth of this word in my spirit, I was able to further understand that God's divine hand is still at work (and that is the blessing of the waiting.) When God opens the door to the season of marriage for me and all who are waiting, He will add no sorrow (as in dread or unnecessary hardship) to it as we trust Him and move in His timing.

My journey of singleness (in the sense of not being in a

committed romantic relationship) was 12 years and 7 months until I entered my previous relationship. This ended because it was revealed that we were not each other's partner in purpose. Before that relationship, I was uninvolved from the age of 23-35 years old. I would meet guys, and I even went out on a few dates, but there was just not that "special connection" that encouraged me to "move forward." Besides that, in other instances, we were just not on the same page about goals, desires and suitability.

As a young girl and a teenager, that "boy crazy" stage just completely skipped over me. I could never understand why some of my female peers were losing their minds (figuratively speaking) about the new guy in class or the popular guy at school. Sure, I thought guys were cute and even liked one here and there, but I was more focused on building my future so that I could be secure in life. As I write this statement, I see how much my father's influence had on me as he would always tell me to stay focused on school so that I would be able to take care of myself and not be at the mercy of anyone. He would also make it clear to me that as my father, after God, he was the only man that was to cover me and that the next after him would be my husband. He would also say that I had plenty of time for guys in my future but, "first things first, please God and get your education."

As I reflect on this, I am so thankful and appreciative of my earthly father's words and affirmation as it saved me from so much. I stand firm today, living in the fruit of his words and instruction. I can also share that through my observation of how he loved and respected my mother and how she reciprocated that same treatment towards him that it set a healthy picture of what a marriage should be. They were both devout Christians. Growing up, I witnessed that pleasing God was made a #1 focus and priority in their marriage.

Because marriage is a God ordained desire of mine, I've taken the time to reflect on my years of singleness. Because we live in a world where people tend to think that something must be indefinitely "wrong" with someone who has been single for a while, some people feel pressured to get into a relationship. They try to "make it work" due to the fear of what others may think.

Just to be clear, it is not necessarily true that something is wrong with a person because they are single and may not have been in a relationship for a while. In fact, there are some people who are currently single because they dare to have healthy standards and refuse to be pressured into being in a relationship that is not God ordained or fruitful. I can personally say that much of my time being single has not been because I didn't have admirers. It's simply because I have not yet been presented by God to my suitable partner. I simply refuse to marry Ishmael when God has promised me Isaac.

I have concluded that when the due season comes, I will meet my tailor-made Kingdom man. I will have no need to question the presence of who he is because it will be confirmed by the peace that God gives which is constant and not the peace that world gives which is fleeting and solely dependent on favorable external factors which are subject to change. I'll also receive confirmation about my Kingdom man's presence by the leading and confirmation of the Holy Spirit.

I know to some that this may sound churchy but, since we are spirit beings called as the righteousness of God, our connections *are* spiritual. As "churchy" as it may sound, I receive the blessings of God that come with it through trust and obedience to Him, His timing, His guidance, and His instruction. Even as I wait (while operating in my life purpose), I truly look forward to connecting with my partner in purpose as it has definitely been a journey. I honestly look forward to the day and onset where we can rightfully submit one to another, honor, love, support, cherish, unite as one, bring forth life and slay the giants of life as we partner in life for the glory of God and reflect His love for the church.

During my wait, can I use my own free will to take matters into my own hands? Of course! But the reality is, nothing fruitful truly comes from operating out of God's timing and taking matters into our own hands. Not only do I know too much about the consequences of doing so, but I also know better. This is not to say that I have not been tempted to do so because I have and even tried to "help" God out in the past at the age of 25.

In my then 25-year-old mind, I felt that if God did not send my husband by the time I turned 30, then it probably wasn't going to happen. My plan was to skip over waiting for God to bring my husband and go straight into motherhood because it was something that I felt I could control. I literally had a real conversation with a male friend at the time who agreed that if I was not married by 30 and if he was not involved with anyone that he would be cool with going through the process of going to a sperm bank (because I was still not open to sleeping with him outside of marriage) for me to have a baby. He also said that he wanted a daughter and felt that I would be a great mother. Although he expressed that he would not be a good husband and did not want to hurt me by engaging in a relationship because of this, he knew that he would be a great father to our child.

Needless to say, I thank God for His divine intervention that allowed me to see the error of trying to "help Him" with the direction and happenings of my life. After processing my decision, God allowed me to see the true intent of my heart and desires and revealed that what I was attempting to do would only render me a fragmented picture of the blessings that He promised me. As I reflected, I also recognized that the basis for me trying to take matters into my own hands was because I did not fully trust God in the area of my love life, and I did not fully understand the integrity of the God that I serve.

I've learned through life and spiritual growth that God knows exactly what we need and the time that we need it. When we're standing in position to receive God's blessings, we do not have to be concerned about the time passing or our biological clocks because the God that we serve is the orchestrator of time and the clock. There may be some people that think that they'll be too old and not have the energy to run behind children if they have them later in age. I feel even stronger that the reason for this thought is because they do not fully understand or trust deeply enough in the integrity of God and even overlook His power because they're looking at their situation through natural eyes.

In some cases, a 40-year-old "may" have less energy than a 25-year-old to run behind young children, but the truth is, God is not practicing when it comes to our lives so He is not going to forget anything that we will need in order to be fit for our blessings. God does not care how "old" we are because He is the bread of life. Our days are in His hands. It is He that will give us the strength that is needed to carry and enjoy the blessings that He is going to give us.

The "timing" of when He may bless you with your heart's desires may not be ideal to you but when you take the time to *really* think about our infinite God and how He works everything out for our good, I'm sure you'll agree. I encourage you to put your list of "must haves" at a "specific" time away and trust the God that gives you breath, life, and purpose to bless you with your heart's desires in His perfect timing. Believe me when I say, God has not forgotten about you. I'm telling you this, not from a place of having received my heart's desire of God ordained marriage, but from a place of waiting as well.

The thing is, we must do our part in being obedient to God's word and get into the right position, place, and posture to not miss or overlook the blessing when it comes. We do this by staying in God's face through prayer, obeying His word and instruction, and using our free will to choose to please Him over man to embark on living a life that is pleasing in His sight. When we fully submit to God, at the perfect timing, when everything is set to His supreme liking (because He sees the bigger picture of our life span and its events), we will receive our hearts desire. The beauty of this is that the time that we thought we lost in the wait on the front end will be redeemed on the back end!

I'm BOLD enough to believe, receive, and stand on this truth. I am not ignorant to the blessings of God or His word when it states that when God blesses a thing, He maketh it rich and adds no sorrow to it. This resonates in my spirit and hopefully yours too. I believe that no matter how long I may have to wait until it's my turn, when it's my turn, God will give me every-thing that I need in order to bask in the fruit of my obedience. I'll be clothed with joy and have happiness as my accessory. I will carry strength and godly wisdom from above to sustain me at my core for life in order to experience the blessings of what I've prayed for. For these blessings, I will not have to compromise my godly standards and the one who God has called to be my partner in purpose will support me in pleasing God before and after we say, "I do" as this will be his determination too.

To be honest, I was not always at this place of fortified confidence in God. There are still times when my faith is tested, but, when I think of how much God has done for me, how He has answered so many prayers, how He saved me from entering into countless toxic relationships, showed me what could have been (through things being revealed), and how He's spoken to me in the moments that I needed it most to affirm that He had not for-gotten about me, I can only surrender to Him in everything!

Hands down, God has been my only proven place of comfort. He has truly been my shield and peace as the fiery arrows of life came straight for my heart yet missed through being in covenant with Him. After days of deep prayer about my longing for relationship and questioning God about my wait, I can remember the moment as I was in my bedroom with the TV blaring that a small, yet loud voice which I knew was God asked me if I trusted him and stated in a questioning tone, "Why would I give to others and not give to you?" That moment of hearing God's voice long ago reminds me even to this day of how much He loves and covers me and has not forgotten about blessing me with His gift of covenant marriage to my partner in purpose.

God wants the best for me, so much to the point where He won't even let me get in the way of His plans for me. Because of this, my confidence rises, and I stand again, unwavering. Besides that, for all reading this book, I want to encourage you to not become envious of the blessings of others. Everyone has a grace. You may look out of your life's window into another's and see something different that appears to be great, and it could very well be. The reality is, for every blessing there will be a certain level of sacrifice attached to it.

A blessing tailored for someone else has a level of sacrifice attached to it that you will not have the grace for because its weight can only be carried by the one it's tailored for. It won't weigh them down and they'll wear it well. This is the very reason why you can know the depths of a person's situation but not see it show upon their face or in their countenance. It's because depending on the issue, they have the grace for what they carry.

The sacrifice may not be sorrowful to the person who may have to carry it out. Again, the only reason why it's not difficult for them is because they have the grace for the cross (weight) that comes with it. Since you do not have your neighbors' grace and they do not have yours, remember that God will give you what's tailored to you in His perfect timing. There is no need to feel or operate in the spirit of jealousy or covetousness. If you do so, you are expressing in the natural and in the spirit your belief that God Almighty has a shortage and is incapable of supplying your heart's desires.

In fact, when we support and pray for those who have received their blessings, especially when they have received what we desire whether it be a spouse, job promotion or the blessing of becoming a parent, we also demonstrate to God that we carry His spirit of love and trust Him to do the same for us. It will be customized for us which makes it even better since we'll be graced for it and will have no sorrow tied to it. Believe it because it's true! If God gives to others, why would He not give unto you?! Trust me, in God, there is no shortage, and you will not die hungry in the wilderness. In fact, as you trust Him, not only will you enter into your tailored promise land but even as you walk through your wilderness, like King David, you'll learn how to praise in the middle of it!

In my season of being in the waiting room to water my own marriage, I continue to walk joyfully in purpose by facilitating health and restoration to married couples and assisting those that are in marriage preparation so that they may make wise and healthy decisions in relationships. Walking in this area of purpose has been extremely rewarding in ways that money cannot buy. Throughout my years of service in the therapeutic field with making my passion of helping others my ministry, I've discovered that God gave me the opportunity to sharpen others as He continues to sharpen me and the King that I'm called to ultimately walk in purpose with.

The reality is, no matter what marital status we are in, there is always so much to learn and walking into the season of marriage does not signify that any of us have "arrived." In fact, when we approach the season of marriage, something new is born which is the reason why it is paramount that we connect with our "partner in purpose." Throughout life, we evolve. With the help of the Lord, our partner in purpose will be able to evolve with us as we grow to be all that God has called us to become. This statement of being in relationship and ultimately marrying your "partner in purpose" is PARAMOUNT to the health and longevity of your marital union and the evolution of one for those reading who are unmarried.

For those who are unmarried and are in waiting, I just felt a nudge in my spirit to inform you that if you do not believe that your tailor-made partner exists, this could very well be a part of the reason for the delay. I say this because God loves to know that we trust Him for our heart's desires to be fulfilled. He finds great pleasure in rewarding those who trust in His integrity.

If we don't believe that it will happen, or that He will not bring it to pass, we put ourselves in a bind both spiritually and naturally. In the spirit, it informs God that we do not trust Him to bless us in this area. In the natural, our negative thinking gives off negative, jaded vibes which could cause us to unintentionally send the message of not wanting to be bothered to a possible suitor or helpmeet.

Am I saying that a person's disposition is the main factor for them not being in a relationship if they are not currently in one? No. But I am saying that it is important to be optimistic spiritually because God will not force anything upon us that we don't have faith to receive. Naturally, it's important to remain approachable (not to be confused with desperate).

This might sound funny, but it's important to not "scowl" on your face because of the message that it may send to on-lookers. It doesn't hurt to smile. A smile should not be seen as an automatic invitation for courtship or interest in pursuing it; however, a smile does send a message that you might be ap-proachable, even if it's just for a "Hello!" The thing is you just never know. Maybe your love story might begin with "Hello." You'll never know if you're not approachable.

It's also important to be interesting and enjoy being your-self. After all, if you don't enjoy yourself as a person, how can you expect anyone else to? If this is an area of insecurity for you, please take the time to invest in yourself by reading the word of God to find out what HE thinks of you such as John 15:9 where it states, "As the father loved me, I too have loved you. Remain in my love." Also 2 Corinthians 5:21 where it states, " For He

(God) made Him (Christ) who knew no sin to be sin for us, that we might become the righteousness of God in Him (that is, we would be made acceptable to Him and placed in a right relationship with Him by His gracious loving-kindness)." I encourage you to read Psalms 139:1-18 also. In my opinion, it is a love letter from God to us depicting how much He loves us, thinks of us and wants to be near us.

God loves you with an unfailing love and you are the righteousness of who He is. If you feel the need to get additional support along with the word of God to help you to begin embracing and discovering your greatness and overcoming impaired self-esteem, I also encourage you to get a Christian counselor. He or she will be able to assist you in working through unhealthy mindsets, learn healthy coping and self-management skills, and overcome past trauma (if needed). The best part of this is that in Christian counseling, you'll also receive help in addressing things of the Spirit through the Word of God and prayer which covers you mentally, emotionally, and spiritually - all of which has a positive effect on your body.

For the person who may have a negative outlook on relationships but happened to pick up this book because it seemed interesting enough, "Thank you." I say, "Thank you," because I want to take this moment to encourage you. No matter the situation, if you have ever been hurt, please know that you are worth your own investment in becoming healed.

You would be surprised at the amount of people that have allowed disappointment in relationships to change them into someone that God never intended them to be. Yes, disappointment and betrayal hurts, but it is unwise to allow anyone that was unworthy of your best in love to change your desire or output to love or be loved. You are better than that, and the love that you have to offer is the answer to someone's prayers.

Have you ever thought that maybe the issue is that you simply gave the *right* thing to the wrong person which *still* makes what you have to give good? Giving a good thing to the wrong person should not make you discard the good that you have to offer. It just means that you have to step back, allow yourself to heal and learn the healthy lesson so that you don't repeat an unhealthy course. In doing so I encourage you to keep moving forward knowing that your merchandise is good!

Remember, your worth can only be appreciated and accommodated by the person that's worthy of it. In God's perfect timing, you will encounter the soul that's meant to intertwine with yours and you will be open and able to receive them because you allowed yourself to heal. When you choose to heal from disappointment, it symbolizes that you refuse to let an unworthy person or situation control or manipulate you into abandoning the goodness that you bring to the table.

Understand that disappointment is not final so please do not park your life there. In the end, as you've taken the time to heal and have learned the healthy lesson, you'll sit across the table from the one that prayed for you to exist, and they will also reciprocate the love that you give. These are the outcomes that we are more likely to receive when we choose to heal and refuse to park in the valley of disappointment.

I pray that this helps you and any man or woman that reads this. It is my heart's desire to see everyone win in love! It is possible for all and is happening every day because God is still giving beauty for ashes. I encourage you to take the time that you need to heal from those past hurts through prayer and or therapy (preferably both) to replenish your soul so that you can become free from cynicism and commit to healthy self-evaluation and reflection in order to see what decisions you may have made that contributed to your heartbreak. Doing so will give you a fair chance at healing so that you can be free to love and accept love from a healthier and wiser place.

You can also fast, pray, and get rid of any items (as appropriate) that remind you of the person or pain that they contributed. In doing so, you will destroy any soul ties that may have been made through your emotional or sexual interactions. All soul ties are not sexual. Some are emotional and can run just as deep.

The Correlation Between Decisions, Happiness and Heartbreak

There is a close correlation between decisions, happiness and heartbreak. Many people would suffer less heartbreak and experience more joy in self and in the fruit of their relationships if they:

1. Incorporated prayer in their decision-making process to seek God's approval first before moving forward into a relationship.

2. Practiced abstinence (for those who are unmarried). It's work but it's worth it!

3. Focused more on their prospect's "character traits" opposed to their appearance and personal "biological clocks."

4. Resisted the trap of falling into peer or family pressure to get married at a certain age, among other things.

5.Capitalized on the gift of being "single" which gives the necessary time to invest in becoming spiritually and emotionally healthy and whole before entering into a relationship.

For you to get a greater understanding of the rationale behind the five points expressed, I thought it would be best to break down each section starting with, "The Benefits of Incorporating Prayer in Your Decision-Making Process While Dating."

The Benefits of Incorporating Prayer in Your Decision-Making Process While Dating

The reason why incorporating prayer into our decision-making processes to seek God's approval before moving forward into a relationship is so essential is because God knows the beginning from the end. Because He knows all things, inviting Him into your decision-making process will reveal things to you that you need to know as well. The truth is, when we're dating, we're going to encounter two sets of people, either the "representative," or the "true self."

The "representative" is the masked version of who you're really getting to know. The thing about this person is that if you knew who they really were without the mask, there's a good chance that you probably wouldn't date them due to the undesirable traits that they may have that would turn you off or be unhealthy for you in pursuing a relationship. An example of someone that displays the "representative" at its finest to lure you into a relationship by not showing you who they really are is a person who is abusive either physically, emotionally, verbally, or mentally.

As a former domestic violence counselor and victim/ witness advocate for the DA office in my city, I can attest that in most of all relationships that encompass domestic violence, survivors have depicted their abusers at the onset of their relationship as being, "Prince Charming" and being everything that they could have ever dreamed. Even though Prince Charming is a man, this does not mean that women cannot be abusive as well. The previous statement is not made to say that all men or women who show traits of being loving and attentive are abusive or have the potential to become abusive, but this is to reiterate the importance of inviting God into your selection and acceptance process **so that you can see deep beneath before you leap**.

Please note that I am in no way saying that it is a survivor's fault for being in an abusive relationship, but what I am saying is that it is important for all people to invite God into everything involving their relationship process. He will reveal things that need to be seen and make it clear if this is a relationship that you should enter or abort the mission to pursue.

The second person that we will encounter as we date is the "true self" which is the person that is truly being themselves from intro to finish. Who you meet and what you see is exactly what you get. This person is consistent in who they're present-ing to you because they understand that the best person to be is themselves. This is the person that is usually very comfortable in their own skin even if it's not popular with the outside world. In other words, this person is not *pretending* to be someone that they are not just to get your attention or affection.

This is the person that you *do* want to date; however, just because you're dating the person that is showing their "true self," does not mean that you have encountered your partner in purpose. What it does mean is that you're getting a more upfront view of what you might be getting into with them while dating them. Either way, it's still important to invite God in, in prayer. It's important because as you do so, God can reveal to you if the person that you're getting to know has good intentions or not,. He shows us if they are "His" best for you *or* not as well as if they are simply your *"assignment"* (someone you're supposed to help grow in God) and not the one that you're assigned to share life with.

With inviting God into your process, you will be given the opportunity to see past the "representative" that many people display when you first meet them when dating. When you're able to see past the "representative" (if they're not showing their true self), you will have the opportunity to see who you're really dealing with opposed to you falling for the masked version that is sent out first to lure you into the relationship because they're either not confident in who they really are and feel that you won't accept them or they're hiding something. Once you're in a relationship with the "representative," he or she falls back into the abyss and the real man or woman runs in to take over from where the representative left off. This is not to say that praying will guarantee a "perfect" person because there is no such a thing, however inviting God into your selection and acceptance process will help you to avoid the unnecessary.

On a personal note, praying and inviting God into my decision-making process with dating has saved me from multiple toxic relationships and interactions. I can remember a time when I was heading into the bank and I met a man in passing who was well groomed but for some reason, I did not want to entertain much conversation with him. It wasn't that he did anything wrong but honestly, I was in a rush and had a list of things to do that day by a certain time and did not want to be stopped.

Because he was persistent in wanting to, "Have a moment of my time and get my phone number" as he stated, to get on with what I needed to do, I asked him for his instead. In addition, I asked him for his first and last name (always get that), along with the correct spelling of it as I entered it into my phone. After that, I went about my day of errands and later that evening when I got home, I said a prayer asking God to reveal to me if I should give him a call and before doing so to reveal anything to me that I "needed to know." After that prayer, I proceeded to do a simple search online.

Lagniappe Note: Because we live in a world where people tend to not inform you of who they really are, it's important to do a little Google search and even check your local sheriff's department online to see if your prospect (male or female) has a record. You would be surprised at the things that people "forget" to tell you. You can also investigate any other background checking programs.

As I put his name in my local criminal sheriff's department website which is "public" information, I discovered that my well-groomed acquaintance was a "John" in a prostitution sting! In addition to that, I discovered that he gave me the incorrect spelling of his name but Google, his social media page and my decision to invite God into my selection process revealed the truth about the spelling of his name as well as his lifestyle, etc. There are more stories that I can tell you, but I think you get the picture.

Sometimes when you pray, as previously mentioned, God may allow you to enter a relationship, however every relationship that He may allow you to enter does not mean that the person that you've gotten permission to date is your life partner. Some people are your lesson to catapult you into passing your test to move into destiny. The key to passing the test is to follow God's will through His word (as you're dating) and learn the lesson so that there is no need to repeat the course.

I was in a relationship where it felt organic and God-ordained because of how well things were going and how we were both believers, practicing abstinence, wanted to please God, liked a lot of the same things, and prayed together, but that relationship ended up being a lesson for me.

As I look back, I'm truly thankful for this experience because I have a greater, more mature understanding of my capacity to love another romantically. Also, my confidence in God increased. I have a deeper understanding of God's will for me in courtship as well as an increased level of spiritual discernment.

Lagniappe Note: Please do not get caught up in the thought that you can tie up God's hands by having high, healthy standards. When it comes to your heart's desires, you are not going to a human with these requests, you are going to God. He is the one who can do all things abundantly!

Your "sound" requests do not scare Him and are not too much for Him. After all, when you desire God's best, He gives you exactly that!! The only thing that I suggest is that you also reflect the sound qualifications of what you desire and require because water seeks its own level. It's important that you meet the standards of your standard. If you do not, then it's time for you to invite God in and get to work in becoming the core reflection of what matters most to you about your desires. You are worth your own investment. Your life outcomes and legacy will be thankful for it.

Overall, incorporating prayer into our decision-making processes to seek God's approval before moving forward into a relationship is essential because God knows the beginning from the end of it. Because He knows all things, inviting Him into your decision and acceptance process while dating and in life in general will reveal things to you that you need to know. The instruction that God gives you along with your obedience will bless you with a greater understanding of knowing both *how* and *if* you should proceed moving forward in a relationship. All in all, your heart will thank you and as long as you stay covered, there will be no need to recover. Prayer saves!

Practicing Abstinence: It Saves Lives, Your Heart, and Time

In today's society, when people generally see the word "abstinence," there are mixed emotions and opinions. Some wonder if practicing abstinence is even necessary to have a healthy relationship that leads to marriage. Others feel that abstinence should be practiced in the early stages of a relationship to see if the person is worthy of their time and body. Some are totally against practicing abstinence and feel that it's outdated and that they must "know" what they're getting into as if sex is the main thing that will occur or matter in their marriage. Some feel as though no one is really "waiting" to have sex anymore and that those that do wait are the ones that eventually get left. Believe me, the list goes on and on.

Whether or not a person practices abstinence or not, the reality is this, giving or withholding sex until marriage will *not* make a person *stay* that wants to leave, and it will *not* make a person *leave* that *truly* wants to stay. Period. The blessed thing about practicing abstinence in this scenario is that if a person that you're dating decides to leave due to you taking the godly stance to practice abstinence in your relationship, everything within you which includes your integrity with self and God remains intact as they walk out of the door.

On the contrary, when the person that you're dating remains consistently supportive of you throughout your relationship as you're both practicing abstinence, there are a few things that you can more than likely be sure of regarding their thoughts of you and your relationship. The first thing that you can be sure of is:

One - they are with you because they really value *"you."* If they didn't, they would not remain with you. We truly live in a world where lust feels like love until it's time to make a sacrifice. When the person you're dating really values you and understands your value, they will support you in pleasing God in the way that you declare is needed. They will make sacrifices and adjustments (as appropriate) because one of the truest definitions of love is selflessness. If you are dating someone that refuses to make sacrifices for you (as appropriate in the season of single-ness) they are not the one that God has ordained for you. When you're dating someone that does support you in abstinence and respects boundaries, you know that you're with someone that truly cares.

Two - they care about your soul as much as you do. The bible speaks clearly about sex not being permissible for those who are unwed because to have sex outside of the covenant of marriage is to "violate the sanctity" of one's own body (1 Cor-inthians 6:18). Sex outside of marriage is considered a desecra-tion against one's own body because of the price that was paid for us through Jesus Christ's blood and death on the cross as the atonement for our sin. In addition, as Believers, we along with our bodies belong to God and not ourselves; therefore, when we allow another to partake in what does not belong to us without God's permission, we are in violation of God's will and His protective parameters.

In other words, when we have sex outside of marriage, we willingly lift the anointed guardrails of protection from over our sacred bodies that was engineered to keep us from experiencing the unfavorable consequences of sex outside of God's protective covenant of Holy marriage. These unfavorable consequences include physical effects (STD's, unplanned pregnancies that cause many children to be raised in single parent homes which can be taxing on both father, mother, and child in various ways and was not God's original design for the family, etc.), mental effects (feelings of depression, shame, guilt, etc.), emotional effects (low self-esteem and emotional restlessness, etc.) and spiritual effects (separation from God due to feelings of shame and regret that cause a person to run from God and anyone that He would send to help aid in recovery among other things).

When dating someone that cares enough about your soul to assist you in pleasing God in your single (unwed) state, it shows their spiritual integrity and commitment. It also sets the platform for you both to focus on fortifying your relational foundation in God and with each other.

Three - they respect your mind and body as well as your commitment to God and see delayed gratification as worth the wait for the blessing that comes with obedience. This is paramount because no relationship stands a chance at survival or thriving without respect, honesty, selflessness and having the ability to see or believe that there is greater beyond the present sacrifice. God is the sustainer and anchor. When you are dating/courting someone that has these characteristics on display and they petition God's assistance in doing so consistently, you have encountered a partner that you can be sure has your best interest at heart and soul.

These are three things in my opinion that you can more than likely be sure of when the person that you're dating remains consistently supportive of you throughout your relationship as you're both practicing abstinence. For those who believe that an individual can be doing all the above mentioned and still have the wrong intentions or be pretending and so on, it's important to remember that when we're seeking God's will, the Holy Spirit will reveal! Of all of the opinions that come, the one opinion that trumps them all when it comes to abstinence is the opinion of God, the one who really "*made*" sex in all of its glory and splendor.

For those who think that God is a prude for instructing His creation to wait until marriage before having sex, please be informed (for some) and reminded (for others) that God put it in His word that after the wait in the premarital stage of a relationship that the reward in their marriage is their marital bed being "undefiled." This means that God endorses and puts His divine blessing on our marital sex life. Who better to put the blessing on our bed than the one who created us, our sexual desires, and everything that encompasses it!!

In the safety of covenant marriage, we have the freedom to be as sexually free and adventurous without need for caution as we explore our spouses' bodies and discover new ways to please one another - as long as it does not include anything that solicits the spirit of lust and perversion. Examples of things that solicit the spirit of lust and perversion that are detrimental to the marital covenant include: inviting others into our marital bed such as having threesomes, watching pornography (which is the exploitation of God's gift of sex, and any other thing that sets the atmosphere to become a breeding ground for perversion.)

Contrary to popular belief, anything that is perverted draws you away from your partner and not towards them due to perversion and the spirit of lust causing you to be enticed by someone or something other than them. When perversion and lust have their way, it causes spouses to have appetites for people and things outside of each other and whenever a spouse has a sexual appetite for anything or anyone other than their husband or wife, believe me, this is dangerous ground and is a set up for marital demise.

Please do not be fooled by mainstream society into thinking that the grass is greener on the other side of perversion and that you're missing something in your sex life (for those who are married) because you're not including lust in it. Lust is actually defined as an unbridled or uncontrolled sexual desire. Anything that is uncontrolled or undisciplined is dangerous because it lacks no boundaries.

Now before you or anyone wants to argue with this, please know that when it comes to spirits, if you allow one that is perverted and demonic in origin to access your life, please know that you in your flesh or your "will" will not have the power to control it. I've heard that sin will take you farther than you intended to go, keep you longer than you intended to stay, and cost you more than you intended to pay. Simply put, it takes the Holy spirit to cast out any stronghold and the stronghold of sexual perversion is included.

Please do not misinterpret what I'm saying and assume that I'm inferring that sex in marriage should be rigid or controlled because that is not the case at all. What I am saying is that unlike sex the world's way that includes lust and perversion, sex done God's way under the protection of His Holy covenant promotes love, euphoria and a God endorsed bond of passion and protection so strong that it draws the marital couple closer to one another in the same way that worship draws us closer to God.

Through the process of worship, we know God more intimately. Through the act of sex which mirrors worship, we know our partner more intimately with detailed knowledge. The grass is deadly on the side of perversion in our marital bed and if a couple gives the adversary an invitation to their marriage, it is hell getting him out because once he is there, his main agenda is to satisfy "his lust" by *not* leaving until the union is fragmented and nearly destroyed if not completely. This is another reason why practicing abstinence and purity in our premarital relationship is key!

With practicing abstinence in our relationship before marriage, we are exercising the power of a sound mind which equates discipline, and this is paramount for success in a marital union. Besides that, practicing abstinence protects you from heartbreak like no other. It sets guardrails to prevent unplanned pregnancy (for the singles), STD's and also keeps us from entering the emotional recovery room due to being wrapped in ungodly soul ties and having to repent from things that we know we should not have committed. There are emotional and spiritual effects in the aftermath when we step outside of God's will.

Practicing abstinence gives you the ability to hear from God concerning *if* you should move forward into marriage with your significant other. Hearing God in this area is imperative because when your marriage goes through a growing pain, you'll be graced for it because you both received God's confirmation on the front end which overall confirms that no matter the difficulties that you face in the middle, you and your love will overcome it and not see divorce as an option.

The key is for both to utilize their free will to remain committed to God and cleave to one another since He confirmed them to become one. To give you more insight on how free God is about us enjoying sex in the confines of marriage, read Song of Solomon in the Bible. You will see how undefiled the marital bed is as both Solomon and his wife expressed their love and sexual desires for one another.

Practicing abstinence (for those who are unmarried) is so important. Not only does abstaining allow you to remain in control of yourself and exercise discipline, but it also makes room for godly discernment to have its perfect way. You will spiritually discover things about the person that you are dating *after* incorporating prayer for God's approval to move forward in dating them.

Because sex is as intimate as worship and is an immediate blinder, when performed outside of marriage, it causes many singles to overlook red flags that would have been obvious if they kept their power by practicing abstinence which allows one to see clear. Lust really does feel like love until it's time to make a sacrifice, but when we practice abstinence and incorporate prayer and fasting, things will be revealed that are imperative for us to see.

For example, the person that you're dating may not be bad, but they may not be God's *best* for *you*. When practicing abstinence, you will not stay in the relationship longer than you need to as things will be revealed to inform you that there's no purpose for you to remain. The scripture that states in 1 Peter 4:8 that "Love covers a multitude of sins" is good overall, but in marriage, it has an added layer in meaning. You get to forgive your partner in their imperfections again and again as appropriate to remain in healthy covenant and in accordance with the word of God.

In the arena of dating, it is also important to forgive, but you *need* to see as much as possible through a sober set of eyes. This is in the natural *and* in the spirit as who you choose and accept as your partner in purpose in marriage plays a big role in your destiny. Please believe me when I say that you "need" to see the red flags and "feel" the uneasiness in your spirit without the strong urge to excuse them.

Whenever we connect our soul to someone though pre-marital sex, we put on blinders that prohibit us from seeing the red flags which are God's warnings before destruction. When we abstain from sex in our unwed state, which also includes abstaining from oral sex, we allow ourselves to see clearly and avoid having countless blind spots that urge us to excuse unacceptable behavior or relationships that do not have God's stamp of approval. When we have sex outside of marriage, we make a covenant outside of God's will with a person that God has not confirmed to us as our partner in purpose.

Because some of us have connected our souls with another prematurely with engaging in sex outside of marriage, this plays a role in much of the reason for resistance and delay in walking away from maltreatment. Having soul ties further explains why It hurts so much when separation becomes undeniable and inevitable.

On the contrary, because abstinence pleases God and our bodies are His temple, practicing it protects our hearts, spirits, souls and bodies by safeguarding us from having to recover from detrimental and unnecessary things spiritually and naturally. In addition to that, abstaining from sex saves us a lot of wasted time by helping us to not spend years with someone who does not have God's approval. Lust coupled with premarital sex can cause you to make spontaneous decisions that have lifetime consequences due to entertaining temporary people that God never intended to stay.

True intimacy starts in the courting process where both parties bring themselves to the table and are open to exploring the mind, emotion and spirit of the other without sexual engagement in the form of intercourse or oral sex. This is done through conversations that include discussing desires, goals, expectations, standards and thought processes on various subjects in addition to spending quality time together, praying and fasting to get God's revelation and clarity, as well as being intentional about fortifying a friendship in the midst.

Lagniappe Note: To all unmarried singles that are dating and are contemplating marriage, please note that red flags during your dating/courting process are God's "clear" signs that you do not have His blessing upon your relationship. This is a major factor that I've noticed that so many overlook only to end up in a sea of regret, brokenness and major despair. Although we do have "free" will, let's make sure that we do not use our free will to "rebel" against God's "warning" signs that are engineered to "protect" our heart's and preserve the "potency" of our legacy. Believe me, what you really want is your marriage to "thrive" and "not" be on life support. With that, it's better to wait for God's endorsement (no matter how long it takes), than to marry wrong and out of season. Especially when it could have been avoided. Where God leads, He feeds!

Because we serve a loving and merciful God, if you have had premarital sex and have found yourself dealing with some of the above consequences mentioned, please know that God is able to restore you, your life, and the lives of your children in such a way that it can seem as though you never experienced the hardship of the events. There is no deficit, pain, or void that God cannot fill as you surrender your will to His so that He can turn your life around and turn what the adversary meant for bad to good in such a way that God still gets the glory from your entire life story through redemption.

How to Abstain From Sex Outside of Marriage (This Section is for Married People Too)

I have absolutely no regrets about my decision to practice abstinence. It has been the greatest weeding out process in the world. When it's come to dating and keeping my purity, sexual integrity and promise to God intact, practicing abstinence has helped me to be able to see what I need to see and hear what I need to hear in order to make wise decisions regarding to my love life. None of my time has been wasted and I've had the luxury of healing from disappointment at a fast rate.

Even when a love interest decided to leave due to not being able to support me in my walk, I lost nothing because everything has remained intact!

With everything shared in the previous chapters, I thought it important to give you information on how to abstain from sex outside of marriage as not everyone is aware of how this is done.

Since adultery is being committed every day, even in the church, I've decided to include my married readers in this section too. Temptation comes for us all, whether married or single.

Since I have been abstaining for many years and the Lord has given me much practice in doing so (don't laugh at me :-), my suggestions on how to abstain from sex outside of marriage are as follows:

1.**Know your triggers.** Ask yourself, "What are the things that make it hard for me to resist temptation?" After you assess your triggers and temptations, ask God to give you the strength and the will to take His way of escape as it appears (1 Corinthians 10:13).

Amid this, deliberately set yourself up for success by setting healthy boundaries. An example of a healthy boundary for those who are single would be to not go by your love interest's home at night or at all for that matter *if* being alone is a trigger for you. Opt for hanging out in public places. This will facilitate more activities where you're out being active as you talk to get to know each other opposed to engaging in activities that are more intimate like a candlelight dinner or activities at night that make it easier for you to go back to your date or significant other's place. I am in no way saying that no one should ever go to their love interest's home; however, I am saying that if going to their home poses a threat to you maintaining your integrity and purity (for both men and women), then you should not put yourself in that or any compromising position that will inevitably cause you to grieve the Holy spirit and lead you to have to repent for actions that you regret.

An example of a healthy boundary for those that are married would be to not allow yourself to be alone with someone that you're attracted to other than your spouse. Being married does not make you blind to the attractiveness of others. If you have to be alone in the office with someone that you find attractive, keep your door open and tell a confidante to check in on you to keep you accountable.

The thing is everyone is in a different place regarding their level of discipline and strength in not being swayed by certain temptations. This is the reason why it is so important for you to be honest with yourself about your limitations and know when you're most susceptible to entertaining or submitting to temptation. A prime example for women is when they're ovulating because biologically speaking, this is when she is most fertile. Because of this, this is the period of the month where her desire for sex is stronger than usual. Although this is not a free pass or excuse to be used to justify fornication, this is an example of the reason why it is important to know thyself and set healthy boundaries. Truth be told, even when a person may have a made-up mind to abstain from sex until marriage, if they put themselves in compromising positions, although they may get away with not submitting to it initially, it is only a matter of time before they will. After all, can a man or woman take fire in their bosom and their clothes not be burned (Proverbs 6:27 KJV)?

It's the same way when it comes to being tempted. If we flirt with temptation, eventually, we'll find ourselves moving outside of God's will towards it and then actively engage with it. I said "moving" and not "falling" because nothing happens outside of the body without it being weighed by our mind first.

First a thought tied to a feeling comes to our mind and then we decide whether or not we're going to move in the direction of our thought and feeling. Besides that, our bodies and our minds speak to us all of the time to let us know where we are on the level of being easily persuaded to go left despite initially wanting to go right. Nothing just "happens" because there are steps that lead up to an action. I believe the reality is that we ignore the signs or overlook them. The tendency to do so is a result of entertaining the flesh and being led by our own lusts. We do this by way of the thoughts that we choose to entertain in private that oppose the leading of the Holy Spirit. Overall, it's important to know your triggers and set yourself up for success by setting healthy boundaries that make moving into having sex outside of marriage more difficult to fulfill.

2.**Date someone that is on the same page with you about prac-**

ticing abstinence. I promise you. This will make your journey so MUCH EASIER!! I do not recommend that you date someone that is not on the same abstinence journey. When you choose to do otherwise you are already unequally yoked due to not being on the same page. Being unequally yoked is not limited to spiritual beliefs. It also pertains to mindsets about core values and suitability for upgrading one another. This means a couple is "better" together than apart.

When two people come together in a relationship, their unity should be so essential to each other's growth and evolution that when they connect, they eliminate the weakness between each other. In the area where one has a limitation, the other has a strength. Since we come together to eventually become one, this is how we are suitable in the fact that we eliminate the weakness between us.

I find it necessary to add that even in the case of a suitable couple coming together, there will still be some conflict because they're coming together to fuse life from different life experiences. The thing is if two people who are suitable can have conflict, this means that choosing to be with someone that is not suitable will warrant even more because there is less room for healthy resolve. Even if you attempt to date someone who was not originally into practicing abstinence but is willing to give it a "try," I encourage you to get permission from the Holy Spirit and not your eyes, which is synonymous to your flesh.

We cannot put God in a box and if this above situation presents itself to you as it may very well likely, please let "God " lead you to and through it, *not* your imagination. In addition, please be clear and inform the person that you're dating of your goal and reasons for practicing abstinence. Express to them that if they are pursuing a relationship with you that you will need him or her to respect your stance and support you in it. This also means that in connecting with you that they too are expected to adopt the stance of abstinence as their own.

It's also important to pray *with* them, *for* them, and encourage them to express their triggers so that you can support them by not tempting them. I suggest that you connect with your Pastors as well as other believers who are on the abstinence until marriage journey as they will be a great support to you and your significant other on your journey and serve as accountability partners. Again, you must maintain your stance and refer back to suggestion **#1** throughout the process.

Whether you're dating someone that was already practicing abstinence or if you're dating someone that is newly practicing abstinence with you, I encourage you to do periodic check-ins to discuss each other's comfort levels, strengths, limitations and boundaries. As time passes, you may find yourself feeling more comfortable with your significant other which can cause you to lower your guard due to familiarity. Please remember that although we do get stronger through the Holy Spirit in reference to being disciplined, we can never trust our flesh because even though the spirit is willing, the flesh is weak (Matthew 26:41 NKJV). This is the reason why it's so important to know your triggers and set yourself up for success by setting healthy boundaries throughout your process. You'll be thankful that you did.

This style of dating with purpose is engineered to assist you in making a wise investment of your time, energy and heart while you are in pursuit of moving forward to the altar without reservation. When dating with purpose in this way, you're setting yourself up to gain as much of the right information as possible about your prospective life partner without making this important decision of marriage through a clouded set of lenses.

Along with prayer, engage in conversation with your partner and interact with each other's family. With doing so and practicing abstinence while dating with marriage being the end goal, you avoid marrying someone that you chose in the dark because everything done throughout your dating process took place in the light which provided clarity. By maintaining your purity, you get the opportunity to assess (without distraction) if your love interest possesses the characteristics needed to sustain and maintain a healthy marital foundation and the marriage that it will be founded upon. These characteristics include but are not limited to assessing if they are of godly character and possess the fruits of the spirit such as love, joy, peace, patience, kindness, goodness, faithfulness, gentleness and self-control (Galatians 5:22-23).

It's also important to assess if you're suitable for one another by sharing the same core values and clarifying if you're equally yoked, which again goes deeper than sharing the same faith. It goes deeper than sharing the same faith because even if we share it, that *may* be the only thing that we have in common and the reality is, sharing the same faith is "not" enough in itself to sustain the waves of life and the course of marriage.

Through my years of prayer, study and observation, I've learned that what sustains a Kingdom marriage is suitability, commitment, spiritual maturity, prayer, friendship, love, trust, sound communication, the use of healthy conflict resolution skills, shared common interests and core values, a healthy sex life, faithfulness, safety in transparency and the studying of God's word as a guide is what keeps a marriage under God's covenant umbrella and ordinance. With being covered by God's covenant umbrella in a Kingdom marriage and exemplifying these characteristics while dating (excluding sex), when the rain and storms of life come, it is this marriage that will sustain every blow and rise above what tries to destroy it.

3.**Get an accountability partner (s)**. An accountability partner is someone or a group of people who know, respect and support you in your goal. In this case, they will support and cover you in your goal of abstaining from sex outside of marriage. They will also strive to not do things or live in a way that will cause you to stumble on your journey as you connect. They will call you out (in love) if you're moving towards doing things that detour you from achieving your goal of maintaining your purity and abstaining from sex outside of marriage.

Abstaining from sex outside of marriage is not limited to staying sexually pure. This also includes not entertaining things that cause your flesh to rise such as actively fantasizing (sexually) about a person that you're not married to. Thoughts come naturally but entertaining them is a choice. It also includes going to strip clubs, "friending" people on social media that you find attractive and entertaining them by sending or entertaining inappropriate DM's as well as hanging out alone with those of the opposite sex. This could pose a threat to your marriage, relationship, or overall goal of abstaining.

Sexual propositions and extramarital affairs occur daily but do not necessarily occur immediately. They occur subtly and those who do not have boundaries in place to protect and maintain their purity and do not remain in prayer or have accountability partner (s), are generally the ones who find themselves most susceptible.

Your accountability partner will be "all up in your business," but not in a judgmental way. They'll be so in a loving way geared to protect you and be another set of eyes to cover you. In many cases, we are unable to see the entire picture because we are in the frame. Accountability partners cover you in areas that you may not have the eyes to see.

Lagniappe Note: When you have God sent accountability partners that you know have godly wisdom and true love for you, please, please, please do NOT push them away because you do not like the truth of what they are saying that opposes the desires of your flesh. Yes, your accountability partner should speak to you in the spirit of love and respect, but sometimes even in love the message must be given firmly.

Sometimes the vision that your accountability partner receives from God comes as His warning and must be spoken in the way that He gives it to them. You will know if a message is from God by the spirit that accompanies the message, and you will know if your resistance to the message being delivered is because of the lust of your flesh. The flesh will lead you to walk *outside* of the will and word of God. Period. The Holy Spirit will lead you to walk *in* the will and word of God with NO compromise. Period.

It would behoove you to adhere to the wise counsel of whom God has placed in your life and not push them away because pushing them away is also symbolic of rejecting the counsel of God. He also works to protect you through the people that He sends to you. You will know who they are by their fruit and the spirit that accompanies them.

Unfortunately, you may also have to "fall back" or separate from your "original" crew of friends if they cannot support your choice of abstinence or godly way of living. I always recommend connecting with someone else that is on the same path as you that can support you as there is strength in a multitude. I've heard and observed that we tend to walk at the same pace as those that we hang with. For example, have you ever walked with someone, and they are walking slowly so you walk "slow" with them but the moment they begin to walk faster you walk faster as well to "keep up?" Well, this goes the same for us about the company that we keep because we tend to walk at the same pace as those that we hang with.

It's an old adage but it still rings true, "If you show me your friends, I can tell you who you are and your character because birds of a feather flock together." Sometimes, though extremely rare, you'll find an exception to the rule, but it is very unlikely and even with that, there is still something within that person at their core that joins them in the company that they keep.

In order to reach a certain goal and in this case, to abstain from sex outside of marriage, it's imperative that you walk with those that fully support you, set a good example for you and have the same goal in mind as together you're stronger. There is safety in a multitude of wise counsel.

4.**Pray, pray and pray.** It's important to invite God into your moments of weakness, you know, those times when our bodies crave sexual intimacy. When you invite God into those moments in prayer, ask Him to give you the strength to be led by the Holy Spirit and not the flesh and to do a new thing within you by stripping away the power that lustful desires have had over you.

This does not mean that you pray and ask God to take away your desire because you will need it for when you get married, and God does not answer that prayer anyway. Trust me, I prayed for it a long time ago and it doesn't work! LOL! But, asking God to assist you in being in control of your desires so that they do not dominate you will work.

After all, our bodies are nothing but a slave to our minds and it shouldn't be the other way around. Whatever you feed the most is what will dominate your thought life so do not entertain things that feed your lustful desires.

5.**Fast and pray**. Fasting and prayer will teach you how to rely on God, His word and assist you in disciplining your flesh by letting it know that the Holy Spirit is what dominates the house (our mind, body and spirit).

Note: When it comes to fasting, you can fast from anything (social media, food, sweets, etc.). God will honor it because the mission behind it will ultimately draw you closer to Him by denying the desires of your flesh and allow you to be yielded to the Holy Spirit. In addition to fasting from a certain thing and praying, it's also important to meditate on scriptures geared to what you're standing in need of. For example, if you're standing in need of mental, physical or emotional healing, one scripture that I would suggest you meditate on three times daily in addition to prayer is Isaiah 53:4-6.

It states, "And he was wounded for our transgressions, crushed for our iniquities, upon him was the punishment that made us whole, and by his stripes we are healed." When you make the conscious decision to fast and pray, believe me, God will reveal Himself to you. What you need, He will supply. When I make the statement that what you need, He will supply, this does not necessarily mean that you will get what you're praying for in the exact form that you ask, but it does mean that you will receive what God sees that you need about your life situation. Sometimes God sees that what you're asking for is exactly what you need and other times He sees that it's not. Either way, whatever you receive from God will be of great benefit to you and it will be what you need.

6. **Do NOT watch certain TV shows where sex is prominent or listen to songs that are suggestive**. You just have to know how much you can handle and stay far from the edge of it lest you become tempted. I also urge you to stay away from pornography of any sort as it will make it more difficult for you to reach your goal of remaining abstinent.

If you must use accountability software to help you to not watch porn, by all means, do so. A simple online search will assist you in finding some. When it comes to suggestive material, it could also be a popular television series or show. Believe me, I know how juicy some of these TV and premium channel series can be but in the grand scheme of things the question to ask yourself is, "Is watching *this* TV show worth the battle of having to fight the flesh after it's over?" Because your decisions count, you must be intentional in making decisions that move you towards achieving your goal and not further from it.

Character, Appearance, and the Biological Clock

W hy is it more important to focus on character traits as opposed to physical appearance and the infamous "biological clock," when determining who you should be dating? The biological clock "may" be a topic of more interest for the ladies but either way you go, this is an important question to answer. Before going straight into answering this question, I feel the need to inform you that focusing more on the qualities that sustain a healthy dating relationship that can eventually evolve into a marriage does not mean that you take the quality of your prospect of having a good physical appearance completely off of the table... (You can sigh in relief now).

Physical attraction is important. You do need to want to have sex with this person among other things, however, let's not confuse physical attraction's importance with thinking that it has to be the supreme basis for the selection of dating and marriage.

I met a man that I was not initially physically attracted to; however, when I got to know him and became more acquainted with his personality, his zest for life and the fact that he was just great to be around, I noticed that I no longer paid attention to the fact that I was not initially physically attracted to him. The truth is, as I got to know him, I saw things in him that outweighed a chiseled body, and a male model's looks. I saw that he was such a beautiful person, comical and here's the kicker, I loved talking to him because he always had something interesting to impart! I can literally remember this like it was yesterday when in the middle of a conversation with him that it hit me, suddenly he became so attractive to me because I saw his heart.

Although he was not my partner in purpose, as I've matured and have developed a greater sense of self-awareness and knowledge about what it truly takes to have a healthy thriving relationship and marriage, I have accepted the truth that with time, looks really do fade and what matters most is a person's character.

Character is one of the many things that will not fade with time. In a world of frauds, when you get the opportunity to meet a man or woman that is authentic in sound godly character, spiritual maturity, faithfulness, integrity, possess a loving heart along with the will and desire to be the best selfless partner possible, and has a great work ethic and the willingness to grow, this person is a blessing standing before you! These character-istics mentioned are but a few of the characteristics that help to sustain a marriage that is rooted in the foundation of God. Point blank, looks can be improved but sound godly character, dignity, faithfulness and integrity as well as the above character-istics mentioned is something (unlike money) that is difficult to manufacture.

In addition to that, knowing where you stand about money is important. Disclaimer: it's important to not put more value on the money that a person makes as opposed to the character that they possess. Money is needed because let's be real, love does not pay the bills and truth be told, romance without finance is a nuisance.

Sounds harsh? I don't mean to sound that way or give that impression but let's be honest, when we do not have the money that is needed to take care of our legitimate needs and purchase even a minimal amount of our desires, it is not only frustrating but disheartening. This frustration and state of being is not the best foundation to build a relationship on, let alone a marriage.

Studies have shown that issues with finances trump infidelity and communication issues as the main factor for divorce. This is in no way dismissing the efforts of any man or woman who is building or who is not wealthy; however, it does shine a light on the fact that money is essential for growth in various arenas and in obtaining the things that we need along with some of our wants for everyday life. Again, romance without finance is a nuisance because if you don't have at the very least the amount needed to sustain yourself, life will be tough and adding a romantic relationship to that will cause more stress due to the requirements that come with it.

The word of God even states in Ecclesiastes 10:19 that money is a defense or an answer to an issue (not to be confused with the love (worship) of money which is the root of all evil in 1 Timothy 6:10). It can be further mentioned that although money is needed, it *can* be made, and money can be made effectively when the individual has the desire to build followed by the determination to take the necessary steps to do so.

We must utilize wisdom and balance in this arena with remaining confident in God first as the source and having money as the resource. This keeps everything in its proper perspective. Although being with someone that you're physically attracted to is good, that quality alone is not solid enough to build a marriage upon and neither is money (in itself) for that matter.

Your "biological clock" should not be a factor in getting married to a person that you have not gotten confirmation from God about. I cannot tell you about the many people in this world that love their children yet greatly "dislike" the person that "they" chose out of haste to create their child's life with. Haste makes waste, and if we are rushing to do something, nine times out of ten we will regret the method that we took to achieve that goal because of the overall outcome.

In hindsight, we discover that if we took the time to think, pray and evaluate our motives for the decision that we were thinking about making, we would not have committed to doing it the way that we did. Honestly, if many individuals that settled for an undesired spouse to start a family spoke their truth, they would encourage you to not make that decision based upon feeling pressured about your "biological clock." They would encourage you to not do this because after it's said and done, you'll still have to live with the good, bad and ugly aftermath after your decision has been made and the clock has ticked. In far too many cases, couples who make impulsive decisions to marry out of haste end up divorced and in many cases their children, unbeknownst to their parents, take on the initial idea that they are to blame for their parents' discord and reasons for separation.

The wise basis for choosing a person to date, eventually marry and build a family with include but are not limited to your genuine attraction to them in ways that are of great value, their faithfulness to Christ (for those who are Believers), their ability to walk in integrity and have respect for themselves and others as well as them having knowledge of their purpose. It's also important that their self-esteem is intact and that they have a healthy ambition, are mentally and spiritually mature and show determination to operate in God's will. Additional qualities include being selfless and not selfish, having good communication and conflict resolution skills (because you and your partner must know how to disagree without dishonoring each other by attacking the issue and not each other), as well as possessing the ability to make wise financial decisions.

Last but not least, another essential quality is being able to provide a safe emotional space for each other to be your most vulnerable self without fear of your deepest expressions being exposed or used against you. The person on the receiving end of these qualities must also reflect and reciprocate these qualities because water seeks its own level. With these characteristics alone, this depicts the reasons why marriage is for the mentally, emotionally, and spiritually mature.

The Importance of Resisting the Trap of Falling into Peer or Family Pressure to Get Married

Society and even some of your family will have you feeling defeated because you're not married. Because of this, if you are not careful, you will fall into the trap of being pressured to marry out of your individual season. You cannot allow societal and familial opinions or your marital status of being single to define your worth and value. God has given you value, and it is He that designs and orchestrates your seasons. No one knows better than Him!

The importance of resisting the trap of falling into peer or family pressure to get married at a certain age, or when you're not ready is because when life happens and you encounter the worst part of "for better or worse", *you* will have to go home to the "worst part" of your marriage, not your family, not society, and not your friends. If you allow yourself to be forced out of your building stage of singleness prematurely, there is a great chance that you'll have to recover from an experience that you were not originally destined to encounter. Need I say more?

The Importance of Capitalizing on the Gift of Being Single and Embracing Healing From Heartbreak

I n today's society, I've come to notice that the state of being single is depicted and viewed two different ways. From worldview #1, being single is viewed as a time to "wild out," and live without inhibitions, doing whatever you want, jumping around and "experiencing" one person after another without penalty or presumed "judgment." From worldview #2, being single is looked at as a negative thing because somehow over time it is insinuated that a person is single because they are not wanted and are falling behind as time goes on; especially if they're not engaging the behaviors in view #1. By the way, it amazes me at how on one end the same worldview that encourages the single (b.k.a the unmarried) to "wild out," is the same worldview that shames, sizes up and looks at that same single "sideways" for following that rule.

When it's all said and done, society hangs them out to dry when the negative consequence of living that lifestyle unveils itself in trauma, impaired self-esteem, STD's, unwanted pregnancies, addictions (both sexual and substance related), depression, anxiety, suicidal ideations, trust issues, and so on. For those who recognize their need to invest in themselves through turning their lives over to God and going to therapy to recover from some of the consequences of their actions, I salute and applaud you because yes, you are worthy and worth the blessing of recovery. In fact, everyone is.

Following mainstream society's worldview on what being single depicts is detrimental. In fact, it's synonymous to watching others walk to the edge of a cliff, see them fall and then go right behind them after you've seen their fate and expect yourself to have a different outcome. It's simply unwise because although recovery is possible, unfortunately, some do not get this opportunity.

The season of singleness from the world's view and God's

design are polar opposites. God's agenda for the season of singleness is to fortify and build the single (b.k.a the unmarried) to a level of greatness with no negative repercussions or unnecessary distractions as the season of singleness is designed to give the unmarried the necessary time to invest in becoming spiritually and emotionally healthy and whole in God and self. This also allows them to discover their purpose in Him before entering into a marital relationship with their partner in purpose for God's ultimate glory.

There are some that truly do not desire to be married because they have the gift of singleness. This gift encompasses the desire and ability to remain unmarried and completely focused on fulfilling God's call on their life and remain sexually pure and content as this also brings God glory. We do not have to be married to bring God ultimate glory because this can also be done without the physical partnership of being married to another person. The one who has the gift of singleness is married to God.

Although opposites attract, familiar/ like spirits connect.

If at our core we are not healthy and genuinely happy within ourselves, we will end up connecting with and accepting someone that reflects our core deficit. This is the reason why doing the necessary self-work is paramount so that you put yourself in position with the help of the Lord to be your best and accept only what reflects "His" best. We will always accept what we feel we deserve which correlates to our sense of self-worth and self-esteem.

At the beginning and end of the day, you deserve God's best. No matter how much time and sacrifice it takes for you to become your best, the end results and the fruit of all of your relationships starting with God, yourself and then others will be worth it! Since every good thing comes from the Father of lights (which is God) James 1:17, if we have a negative, doubtful attitude and do not believe that our tailor-made suitor (for my sisters) or help meet (for my brothers) exists, then as mentioned before, we're also inadvertently expressing to God that we do not trust HIM to provide in the arena of our love lives.

One thing is for sure, God will not force a blessing on anyone, and He won't give a whole person to a broken person as the broken person that is still consumed by pain cannot accommodate the needs of *or* do life with someone who is whole for, they are unequally yoked. Anyone who is still dealing with the pain of heartbreak would not be able to maintain a healthy relationship anyway because they'll question the integrity of their partner to no end. No one who is emotionally whole will entertain this behavior for long.

It's very important to invest in your own healing after heartbreak to avoid having the pain of cynicism direct the course of your love life. Healing involves two things. One - being truthful to yourself about your emotions and the pain that you experienced. Two - taking the time to reflect on the incidents that occurred to have a better understanding of what happened and what was said by both parties in order to process the event so that you can identify what you can do differently moving forward.

No matter the incident, the only person that you have the power to change is yourself. Even as you do this, don't reflect to pass blame. Reflect to assess how you can make better moves moving forward. After reflection has been done, it's imperative that you process the steps that you will take in order to recover. These steps should include prayer and running to God as your safe place to recover, journaling (if need be) because it's therapeutic and allows you to see yourself from the outside as you read what you wrote, and also therapy (if needed). This helps you to further put the pieces together to move forward in a healthier way and help you to unpack unhealthy thought processes.

Entertaining the Bad Boy/ Bad Girl Type

Everyone likes someone with a little edge. I get it! Everyone needs love. I get it! It's not a question or debate about if everyone deserves love, it's a question about "who" deserves "your" love. When it comes to bad boys and bad girls, I have to let you know that entertaining a relationship with a person that is hot tempered, easily angered, and who refuses to follow the rules is synonymous to putting your literal heart in the hands of someone that is on fire!! Get that image in your head... Got it yet?... Now, ask yourself (with still having this image in your mind), "Would a person ablaze be a safe person to place my heart in the hands of?" With that same image in your mind, what do you think is going to happen to your heart if you place it in the hands of someone on fire?? You guessed it, your heart will be set on fire and burned alive too! I don't know about you, but to me, that's a disturbing image to see, even if only in my head.

For my ladies, I get that we may want a handsome man with some spontaneity, a little mystery, breathtaking masculinity, and even for some, a little "street credit" to feel that they're protected. For my brother's, I understand that you may want a "baddie," with an Instagram model body. You may even want her to have some street credibility among other things that blow your mind and peak your "levels" of interest. For both sexes (Genesis 5:2), the above-mentioned qualities are indeed ego boosters. They may even get the adrenaline pumping. Even so, believe me, "prioritizing" the things that I've mentioned above only provides a false sense of security and sustainability. They do not provide, nor should it be put in place to guarantee positive outcomes when it comes to building a legacy that your children can thrive on!

When a person is unable to control their temper, is easily angered, and cannot self-regulate or even care to think about the consequences before they act, it is a sign of emotional instability which is a dangerous place to consider investing your heart, let alone your legacy. Any person that is unstable or prone to sudden change, no matter how dressed up or fancy they are is a liability. If instability is their baseline, the smallest thing that makes them feel threatened or uncomfortable will cause them to break at the seams at the slightest touch. What is unstable cannot be easily managed. You will have consequences that you did not initially bargain for. Furthermore, he or she that is easily offended is easily broken.

Hot tempered people are people who usually think irrationally and have unaddressed trauma and insecurities which are the reasons for their unhealthy behaviors. This is not mentioned to put anyone down that has experienced trauma because we all have trauma in some form. The issue is that for those who are quick tempered and angry, they've allowed their trauma to consume them which is why they're on fire most of the time or a second from being so in the right setting. Either way, placing your heart in the hands of an angry person is unwise.

The Bible even tells us in Proverbs 22:24 "to not make

friends with an angry man and with a furious man do not go unless we learn his ways and set a snare for our soul." With this, if God tells us to not make friends with an angry person, what do you think His thoughts are about getting into a romantic relationship with one? For my men, do you think your legacy (children) are safe to be placed in the womb of an angry woman? For my women, do you feel that you would want the seed of an angry man placed in your womb?

When it comes to relationships, there is a lot to think about that goes far beyond swag, guts, aggression and a nice build, frame or smile. As mentioned before, this does not mean that you will have to forfeit physical attraction to get a good spouse because there are highly attractive individuals who have great qualities that will not cause you to be in the position of picking up the pieces. This is expressed so that you keep the bigger picture in mind. Do not allow the flesh and things that are superficial or unwise to potentially cause you distress in the long run. Superficial focuses merit nothing at the end when it comes to building life and wealth.

Preparing for Marriage

P rior to marriage, in order to bypass the extra work to build a healthy marriage, it is important to keep some things top priority. A major priority is to have a solid, yet ever evolving personal relationship with God. It's also important to be healthy in mind, body (the areas that we can control) and spirit. We must remain active in continuous pursuit and maintenance of that.

Self-awareness and knowledge of your purpose - or at the very least having a general idea of it in order to connect with your partner in purpose - is also a major key. This is a component of what couples in marriage should represent. After all, if one can put 1,000 to flight and two can put 10,000 to flight as stated in Deuteronomy 32:30, this signifies that coming together is engineered to make us better and stronger in pursuit of all that we're called to obtain and have dominion over.

I like to equate marrying your partner in purpose as walking in God's purpose of oneness by exemplifying Christ's love for the church. I think it's also worth mentioning that in preparation for marriage, if you're dating a person who is not willing to pray, that is a sign of spiritual immaturity. This is an area that you want to discuss. Yes, everyone is at a different level in their walk with Christ; however, if this person is not actively seeking to grow spiritually, sloooooow down and pump the brakes! Please make a mental note that even salt looks like sugar. This means that you cannot make an accurate assessment of a person based upon appearance alone. Look deep before you leap and if a person refuses to go deeper with you in the spirit, it's a sign that they're not ready to embark on a Kingdom relationship that leads to a Kingdom marriage.

Another thing to keep in mind is to be cautious of those who are more open to revealing their accolades (accomplishments) but over time are still resistant to reveal things that require them to be more vulnerable as appropriate. When you date to marry a person, in the long run you are not going to be building life with their accolades, you'll be building life and living with their spirit and mindset and everything that accompanies it. This includes their checked and unchecked experiences, both negative and positive.

Am I saying that people should reveal everything about themselves in the initial dating process? No, because it's a process, but what I am saying is that over a course of a few dates and multiple conversations in between that both parties *should* know more than surface information about each other and continue to reveal what's needed as time progresses; especially if they're both being intentional in building a healthy thriving relationship and friendship that leads to marriage. After a certain point if a person refuses to discuss things beyond surface level topics, this is a sign that they're either hiding something or have trust issues which are two things in which a healthy relationship cannot evolve constructively from.

Because it is imperative that we prepare for marriage **before** we get married, I've taken the liberty to single out a few areas that need to be discussed in detail such as:

1. The importance of facing *your* issues

2. Addressing the spirit of lust

3. The importance of being *selfless* and *not* selfish in marriage

4. The importance of setting healthy boundaries

5. The importance of financial stability and love

6. The importance of *healthy* communication and conflict resolution skills

Are you ready to prepare for your marriage? If so, turn the page and let's get to it!

Face Your Issues: Single Issues Become Marital Issues

I t is very important to address the issues or baggage that you have as a single before entering marriage. This is something that one too many couples gloss over in order to run into the fantasy and romanticism of marriage. One thing is for sure, if you gloss over the issues that you have, they will definitely re-surface right after the honeymoon is over.

I've come to recognize that marital issues are really single issues that were not appropriately, if at all, addressed. Whatever issue we have in our unmarried state that we do not address and overcome will unfortunately be magnified in our marriage. It is our marriage that will take the hardest hit. In other words, any giant that you do not slay while single will become a giant that you and your spouse will have to slay in your marriage.

If you both do not have the tools to slay the giants that come to challenge you, your marriage will take the hardest hit.

For example, if in our unmarried state we have issues with insecurities within ourselves and trust issues with others, these are issues that will inevitably plague our marriage due to cynicism becoming the lens that we see our world and others through. Whenever a person is insecure, they have a great tendency to treat their partner as a prisoner and they themselves in turn become the warden. Because of cynicism and insecurity, they may also see their partner as a potential threat to hurt them. Their past experiences could further fuel the unhealthy desire to imprison and accuse them by making them take charge for a crime that they did not commit.

Just like the previous example, insecurity of any form for that matter is an unhealthy trait to have in a relationship, especially for one in which both parties desire the relationship to thrive. Whenever trust issues and insecurity become the lens or checks and balance of a relationship, the relationship is doomed. At the point when doomsday comes, this couple must look at the part that they both played in its demise, seek to correct it or be forced to repeat the course - even if in another relationship - if they haven't learned the lesson. This is why I encourage everyone to seek individual therapy and counseling in order to address the issues that they know have caused them distress. Therapy will also assist individuals in uncovering the blind spots or the problem areas in which they had no idea were existent.

Whenever we do not address an issue that needs to be resolved from a previous relationship, when a conflict arises that reminds us of the unresolved painful experience, it can cause us to try to make our partner take a charge for a crime that they have not committed. It is this type of behavior that can promote the death of the relationship if the real facts and issues are not presented and addressed. When issues such as insecurity and distrust are meditated on, not only do we stay imprisoned by the event, but we in turn make others that we're connected to become imprisoned to our pain as well.

Since familiar spirits are attracted to one another (even if it's shared brokenness), whatever state we are in, we will automatically connect with someone who also has that dominant spirit (whether good or bad). It can be further mentioned that some people hold onto the memory of an offense by thinking that if they constantly rehearse or remind themselves of it that this will keep them safe from the pain of experiencing it again. This could not be further from the truth. In fact, by holding onto pain, you victimize yourself again, again and again because each time you replay the offense, you experience the hurt and therefore relive the trauma.

Although your pain might parade itself as anger, at its core, underneath the anger resides hurt and pain, nonetheless. I truly believe that the reason why people in general are quick to display anger opposed to hurt is because the hurt individual does not want to appear "weak." Since anger is seen as powerful and power is to be "respected," this is why people are more open to show anger when what they are really experiencing is pain, disappointment, etc. Even so, if we continue in this behavior and never address the *real* issues to embark upon healing and restoration, the only thing that we can be sure of getting is "re-infection." The truth is, when something hurts deeply, you don't forget it but the way to heal the wound is to get the care that you need. Although there may be a trace of a scar, the area will no longer hurt to touch and if anything, you'll have a story to tell of how you healed which can help to save someone else.

Addressing the Spirit of Lust: The Consequences of It Going Unchecked

Another very important subject to address that goes majorly overlooked, either due to society's unhealthy norms or out of plain ignorance is the subject of "lust." I cannot tell you enough about the importance of addressing the stronghold of lust before you get married. You may think that issues of lust may not pose a threat to your marriage, but they will. Whenever the spirit of lust is tolerated, the spirit of perversion has a foothold in to eventually run the show and run your marriage into the ground.

Our marriages are supposed to exemplify Christ's love for the church. With this being said, because of what marriage represents and the holiness and power that it embodies as we connect with our partner in purpose, it is an automatic threat to the adversary. Just as Adam and Eve's coming together represented life being lived unified and abundantly and because the devil saw the power in it, he came cunningly as a snake in the grass, appearing harmless because of his subtle approach. Lust comes in the same way and just like the devil in the form of a serpent in the garden, it has no limits. In fact, just like the snake in the Garden of Eden, it appears as though it's supposed to be there.

Let's be honest, today and even in the societies before today, lust takes on the appearance of excitement and comes dressed cunningly and promising fulfillment into things that you've never imagined. When you touch it and invite it in, it fills you with a rush like a drug for the first time. Lust infiltrates your cells and seeks to infect the legacy in your DNA through generational curses. You can find yourself going back, wanting more and more, never being satisfied because lust makes promises that it cannot keep! In fact, it sometimes shows up and feels like love because of its intensity, but it is revealed as the fraud that it is when it's required to make a sacrifice.

Love is selfless and lust is selfish. Lust is rooted in perversion and deception, is self-seeking and only stops when it has destroyed its host and almost everything that the person has built. Lust has brought many men and women to their knees in shame and demise due to the collateral damage that have resulted in broken families, ransacked lives, destroyed empires and more that date back to biblical times. This is exactly how generational curses form through doors that were not secured and ultimately were overlooked or unaddressed that allowed perversion access.

An example of how unaddressed lust can corrupt a marriage is that it can cause consistent wandering eyes and also issues of intimacy. When a person has not purged their spirit of sexual encounters and the thoughts that come with it like the way that a past sexual partner performed, it does not give room for a person's spouse to be the source of sexual fulfillment. Their unchecked lustful thoughts, sexual appetite, and needs to reach orgasm from being with a past partner clouds the person's psyche. Because of this, pressure to perform can be placed on one or the other individual. This does not allow them to experience love making as a fun, uninhibited exploration of each other's bodies but rather the chore of being able to "be good enough" or "better than" the previous partners.

The reality is, sexual acts performed or done outside of God's will should never be compared to sexual acts committed in His will because an act performed in an unholy setting should never be placed on the same pedestal as an act done in a holy one. This does not mean that sex in covenant should not be mind-blowing due to it being endorsed by God, in fact should be even more PHENOMENAL because the MOST High is blessing it! Sex outside of God's will should NOT be better than sex in His will! For those of you who are married, by all means live and liven up your sex life to the fullest because you've got GOD'S stamp of approval on it!

It can be further mentioned that when lust is not extinguished, it makes infidelity convenient and easier to commit in the mind of the one who commits the act because they will find multiple reasons to justify the act and have no boundaries set in place as a guardrail. If lust is an issue that deals with *you*, I encourage you to deal with *it* by committing this spiritual stronghold over to God through prayer, fasting, sealing up all doors where lust can enter such as through pornography or other suggestive material. I also encourage you to stay accountable to those who can help you to overcome this issue regarding informing them of your whereabouts, separating yourself from people, places or things that make indulging in lustful acts easy, as well as going to counseling to get to the root of the issue.

Because any spirit that we feed the most is what will dominate us and anything that is not fed will die, I encourage you to work on starving the spirit of lust because it will do no service to you, whatever you're seeking to build and fortify, especially in relation to your current or future marriage nor will it please God. Although you may not think of it initially, God invented sex, not man. Don't you think that the one who designed, developed and put a name and purpose to sex knows exactly how to assist you in having the greatest sex of your life with the one whose body He also designed, especially for you?

God in all of His power created sex to bless and not destroy. When we allow perversion to enter, it goes against the very origin of God's creation for sex. Trust me, the BEST sex to have is LOVE making where a married couple is able to be completely naked, vulnerably safe, loved, cherished, and made the only star of each other's midnight, morning, daytime and midday show. As they renew their commitment to each other through love making, this further conveys to the couple involved that they only have eyes for each other and that their mind, heart and spirit is set on pleasing and recommitting to each other based upon what they've learned from exploring the gift of each other's body, mind, and soul as they connect as one.

Be Selfless, Not Selfish

It's also important to be selfless and not selfish (as appropriate). When I make the statement about the importance of being selfless and not selfish in a relationship, I recognize that not everyone understands the true concept or definition of selflessness and may interpret it as taking on the stance of being a doormat and not speaking up about your needs. This couldn't be further from the truth. Selflessness can be defined as, "being more concerned with the needs and wishes of others than with one's own." In this case, you would be selfless towards your partner and this behavior truly exemplifies what true love is and what it encompasses.

In a healthy relationship and marriage, the behavior of being selfless (as appropriate) is not one sided because both partners are selfless towards one another. When couples operate in the manner of selflessness, they both end up winning in their relationship. Each person is heard, and their needs expressed.

There will be adherence to or at the very least their partner will strive to meet that need to the best of their ability (as appropriate depending on their marital status). This is essential to the health of any relationship.

On the contrary, the opposite of being selfless in which being *selfish* is defined as "lacking consideration for others and being concerned chiefly with one's own personal profit or pleasure." The characteristic and behavior of being selfish goes completely against what love is. According to scripture in 1 Corinthians 13:4-7 it states, "Love is patient, love is kind. Love is not jealous or boastful or proud or rude. It does not demand its own way. It is not irritable, and it keeps no record of being wronged. It does not rejoice about injustice but rejoices whenever the truth wins out. Love never gives up, never loses faith, is always hopeful, and endures through every circumstance."

Let's bring some clarity and balance to this scripture because there are some (out of ignorance, selfishness or both) who have twisted this scripture to manipulate, control and emotionally abuse their partner. First and foremost, this scripture implies the love of Christ who went to the cross for us. He, who was without sin, was only able to stand proxy and die for us because of God's love. This love as described in 1 Corinthians 13:4-7 is the full manifestation of how God desires us to love and treat each other (mutually) by following Christ's example. Christ's life alone was the true example of selflessness and because marriage reflects Christ's love for the church, it is a mirror that will cause God's characteristics of love to surface in all of us as we are being proven and tested in our union to love like Christ through the hills and valleys of life.

Although marriage will cause us to exercise these characteristics of love, this does not in any way give anyone a license to deliberately abuse the grace and love of another and feel that their partner is mandated to accept abuse in any form for the sake of the relationship. Love does not cause pain and does not seek to abuse or manipulate. It can be further mentioned that although people are not perfect and we are all under construction (just in different areas), we should pray and partake in self-evaluation before getting into a relationship or marriage.

Everyone should ask themselves if they truly have the capability, capacity, and characteristics of being selfless. If they answer "no" after truthful and honest inspection, a relationship and marriage is *not* the journey that they should embark upon at this time. For the individual with a selfish mindset, proceeding with a relationship or marriage (at this time) would be synonymous with them walking into failure. They don't have the appropriate mindset and spiritual maturity that is essential in having a healthy relationship or thriving marriage. This is in no way stating that this person will nct get there at some point, however, respectfully, the time is not now. If they do so anyway, their relationship, marriage and all involved would in more cases than not end up becoming collateral damage.

Setting Healthy Boundaries and Utilizing Discipline

While in high school I learned a quote that has never left my spirit. It states, "Discipline is the training that makes punishment unnecessary." It is important to be able to set and maintain healthy boundaries with self and with others. Exercising discipline helps us to avoid walking into temptation's traps. With this being said, in life and within romantic relationships there will be many temptations but setting healthy boundaries (lines that you will not cross) and exercising discipline (restraint) is what will keep you and your beloved from having to deal with the painful emotional consequences of them being hurt and you knowing that you are the cause of their pain which would be emotionally punishing for you both.

Please note that all temptations are *not* sexual. Some temptations take on the spirit of a person being tempted to tell lies due to the fear of punishment or being a disappointment if the truth is revealed. Others are tempted to entertain a rebellious spirit and do things their *own* way despite wise counsel that advises otherwise. Then, there *are* others that allow themselves to be tempted by the lust of their flesh by telling themselves that they can entertain flirting with someone other than their significant other and not get caught.

If you have mastered and continue to actively maintain the spirit of discipline (which God has given us the spirit to do in 2 Timothy 1:7), temptation will not easily overtake you. With each test that you pass (because you will be tested), you'll give the devil a black eye. One thing that people can use to gauge where boundaries should be set is to identify the things that you would not want exposed and set restrictions to help you to avoid engaging in the activities that would reap that outcome. When we work on mastering a sound mind (which equates to discipline) we avoid the feelings of shame and backlash that indulging in temptation would involve before and in the event of exposure.

The thing that I want you to remember is that in setting healthy boundaries and in utilizing discipline, you are not alone in this. You are not to assume that setting these boundaries and being successful at attaining the goal of being disciplined is all on you. God is here to help you set yourself up for success, and the Holy Spirit will back you up. Ways to master the spirit of discipline are to pray and ask God to give you the ability to draw from HIS strength to operate in a sound mind and to receive the power of godly discernment. Ask God for His help in assisting you in practicing delayed gratification by setting a goal and writing smaller goals or sub steps that will help you to achieve the larger goal and stick to the process.

It's also important to have accountability partners, engage in positive self-talk, state positive affirmations daily that refer to you completing the task at hand and read scriptures like Proverbs 16:3 where it states, "Commit your work to the Lord and your plans will succeed," and Galatians 6:7-9 where it states, "Don't be misled, you cannot mock the justice of God. You will always harvest what you plant. Those who live only to satisfy their *own* sinful nature will harvest decay and death from *that* sinful nature. But those who live to please the spirit *will* harvest everlasting life from the spirit. So, let's *not* get tired of doing what is good. At just the *right* time we will reap a harvest of blessings *if* we don't give up."

Whatever spirit or ideas that you entertain the most, (be that of the Holy spirit or the temptations of the flesh) will be the one that has the most power over you. Utilizing discipline and setting healthy boundaries with God's help are two *major* keys that will help to prepare you for marriage and could protect it. Since preparing for a healthy and thriving marriage is the goal that I'm sure you have, the above-mentioned keys are surely the ones to choose. The blissful longevity of your marriage and all that will be birthed from it will thank you.

Financial Stability and Love

L earning the art of financial stability and being a wise steward of the finances that God has afforded is foundational. It is important to be in position to increase it or at the very least be in motion to do so. It can also be mentioned that it is better to be wealthy than to appear wealthy and not have the finances to back it up. With that, it is so unfortunate that we live in a world where one too many spend more time on looking like money compared to having it.

Am I saying that everyone must be a millionaire? No, but what I am saying is everyone should do their best to strive to be as financially savvy and affluent as they can in their own right as well as exercise wisdom in their youth so that they do not have regrets in their later years. Besides that, being financially stable affords us the luxury of providing not only for the needs and wants -within reason- for ourselves, our family and children, but we will also have the opportunity to help and teach others that may have experienced hardships to become self-sufficient as well.

Please don't take this the wrong way, but the truth is, romance without finance is a nuisance because love does not pay the bills and the lack of finances guarantees an increase of discontentment at some point. Because of this, it's important to evolve in the area of exercising financial wisdom and exploring the art of having multiple streams of income so that you may leave a legacy of wealth for the next generation.

I hear some people argue that the lack of finances should not be the reason why a person does not marry and to some degree, I agree. However, I must state that no matter how much you may love a person, the truth is, once again, romance without finance is a nuisance because of the distress of what the lack can cause. Although love is wonderful and much needed, it alone cannot be the basis of sustaining a marriage and family. In the same breath, money alone cannot be the basis of sustaining it either.

My point in this matter is that romantic love and money can mix well and both individuals involved in the relationship/ marriage should have financial goals. If they have not yet attained it, they should at the very least be actively moving towards financial stability without unnecessary excuses. I especially encourage those who are young and do not have the responsibility of parenting to seize the moment and utilize their youth wisely so that when they approach their 30's and are into their 40's, they can parent and make affluent decisions for their children with greater financial grasp. When it comes to marital longevity, commitment to GOD, each other and *then* love and romance is the order of sustenance. Physical attraction (in many cases) is important because that is what initially attracts us. Putting love last on the list of 3 things that sustain a marriage (although there are more) may come as a shock to some. The reality is people are falling out of love and romance every single day. Besides that, many people that have experienced divorce or are currently going through a divorce *still* love and care for one another. This means that if love and romanticism was all that it took to sustain a marriage, then there would be no divorces and certainly no reason for me to write this book.

Although opposites attract, it is what we have in common that keeps us together. This is the reason why it is paramount, once again for us to marry our partner in purpose and be equally yoked. Our partner in purpose is the person that will evolve with us as they are our suitable helper and capable of going through our stages of evolution with us in grace and vice versa as we continue to make our marriage and communicating with one another a priority along with remaining a student of one another. Together, suitable partners assist one another in the fulfillment of their God ordained purpose on earth. When you think of the power of this kind of union, it would behoove us to not settle for less than God's best and trust Him through the process of connecting us with our partner in purpose.

Healthy Communication and Conflict Resolution Skills

When it comes to conflict and healthy communication, it is important to know that assumptions will always "kill" what "sound" communication can save. Disagreements are inevitable in even the best of relationships, however, knowing how to resolve your issue is even more important than what your issue is about. The main thing to know is that when in conflict, it is imperative that you "attack" the "issue" and never your partner!

When we form relationships, we become allies (people of safety). Whenever we choose to attack our partners (our greatest allies), it weakens the structure and depth of our relationship as well as damages our relationship's foundation. After all, "real" war (issues) is a part of life. If your partner sees that you're liable to switch sides in battle and attack him or her as opposed to the issue, how can they *truly* feel secure and trust a supposed "ally" (person of "safety") who turns on them? Although forgiveness is necessary, *forgiveness* and *trust* are two *"separate"* things. The moral of this illustration is to attack the issue *together* and *not* turn on your partner. If you choose to attack your partner you've given place to the enemy. If the adversary is not properly rebuked, your relationship with your partner as you once knew it will only be a memory and allies you will be no more - even if you decide to exist together despite the trust between you being broken.

In order to avoid the above-mentioned outcome and maintain a healthy relationship and marriage, I encourage you to develop healthy communication and conflict resolution skills before and during your relationship and marriage. For those who are unmarried, I encourage you once again to wait until you have received God's clear confirmation that you've met your partner in purpose in order to proceed moving forward in matrimony. Even married couples who are called by God to be together will have areas of conflict that they will need to resolve, but through God's grace, they will be able to resolve those areas despite moments of difficulty. In fact, the confirmation that they received from God to get married is what will help them to proceed in confidence that all will be well on the other side of their trial as they both continue to submit to God's will.

If a couple called together by God will have moments of difficulty, just imagine how difficult the conflict will be to navigate if you marry someone in which God did not give His blessing to move forward with? The funny thing is, with all that has been mentioned thus far, this has not even scratched the surface of what it takes to sustain a marriage. This statement is not intended to scare anyone but to simply inform them that marriage is serious. It is a covenant that we make with God and our spouse that is intended for life. Even still, constant fellowship with God from both individuals and having wise godly counsel both in and out of church, and therapy (even when nothing is wrong) are practices that make having a rock-solid marriage attainable. In addition to that, maintaining a teachable, forgiving and selfless spirit, having healthy communication, and maintaining fidelity are characteristics that will fuel the longevity of your marriage.

I cannot tell you the countless marriages that ended before they even began due to the deficit of not having the previously mentioned variables addressed. I've witnessed that in today's society, more emphasis and interest is placed on preparing for the wedding *day* compared to marriage itself. As a society, more money is invested in preparing for the wedding ceremony compared to preparing for marriage. This is a reason for the decline of thriving marriages. It would amaze you to know the amount of people that are *still* repaying loans for the wedding day of a marriage that they are no longer in.

Contrary to popular belief, the institution of marriage is *not* the issue, the unprepared state of mind and spirit of those who entered is! Some may say that they went to premarital counseling with their Pastors before they got married so that should have been enough, right? Wrong! Effective premarital counseling takes much more than three meetings where 9 times out of 10 the betrothed couple will not discuss their *real* issues or concerns with their Pastor due to wanting to maintain an image for them *and* the fear of their Pastor informing them that they're not ready for marriage if they were completely transparent. Besides that, I've even heard that *some* Pastoral premarital counseling sessions only entail a reading of scriptures on marriage, the explanation of them and then the couple being asked if they understood what it meant. Of course, more than a handful of these couples will state "yes," to get the show on the road!

I am in no way discrediting premarital counseling with our Pastors as my future beloved and I will definitely meet with ours before our wedding day. What I am saying is that premarital counseling should be done before the "will you marry me" question is popped. This allows you to gain more wisdom and insight *or* at the very least months before you meet with your Pastor ensures that the areas of importance are addressed and assessed so that when you do meet, you do so with all confidence that as many bases as possible have been covered. This allows you to walk in greatly advised and equipped for your Pastoral premarital sessions.

Three Reasons Why Relationships Fail #1: Ignorance

Having practiced for 15 years as a counselor/ therapist, I found that there are three main components of why relationships fail. These components include either: ignorance, negligence, the relationship not being God ordained or all of the above. Ignorance can take on various scenarios. I'll start with this scenario - when one or both partners are unaware of the blessed characteristics that they have in their significant other and take his or her existence, heart, and sincerity for granted. One or both partners may take the other for granted and begin to feel that there is someone "better" or able to provide more "excitement" than their current partner. I understand that sometimes the individuals in a relationship are not suitable for one another, as in "the best fit" (partner in purpose) for the evolution of each other's lives, however; what I've come to consistently observe is that when the partner who decides to leave due to feeling that the grass is greener on the other side realizes that the grass isn't so green, they get this "unforeseen" epiphany that all that they really wanted in a relationship was what they already possessed. With this, they sometimes go to various lengths to get back with their previous partner. The old adage really is true when it states that hindsight is 20/20. Unfortunately, by the time an epiphany is reached, in some cases the partner who was invested in the relationship has had time to process the pain and details of the relationship and because they know their value and trust has been broken, a wall is erected that, in various cases, does not permit reconciliation.

In my opinion, reconciliation should not take place in this situation *unless* the Holy spirit leads one to do so. I state that reconciliation about resuming the romantic relationship should not be the immediate response because we teach people how to treat us by what we accept or tolerate. Sometimes our significant others do not leave on their own accord. Sometimes they leave because God moved them. Yes, I said God. God sees the beginning from the end. Even when a relationship starts good and is good throughout the first 6- 9 months, it does not necessarily mean that this is the person for you.

Once again, for my unmarried readers, confirmation from God is key before proceeding into marriage. God sees the full picture. He causes some relationships that seem good to end. He can see what you may have to endure 10 years down the line, which may not be His will or His best for your life. There are things that God knows that remain a mystery to us. Who's to say that your previous partner has really gained revelation and a great respect for who you are and what you bring to the table? Who's to say that their return is not because of a selfish motive - where returning to you only serves *them* due to the comfort that you bring to their life (that they are not capable of reciprocating) and could not find in another? In some cases, people take your love for them for granted and believe that you love them so much that after they leave to be with someone else (because they know that you wouldn't tolerate infidelity), they bank on you taking them back. This perception is one of selfish motives founded on self-seeking ground. Healthy love cannot be built or sustained in this type of environment.

My advice to anyone who is sincerely contemplating leaving their partner due to thoughts that the grass is greener on the other side is to seek wise counsel through therapy (both individually or as a couple) or through a trusted, proven individual (with a sound track record) before making this potentially permanent decision. Things are not always as they appear because even salt looks like sugar.

On the flip side, if you know in your spirit that the person that you are with is not the person for you, please do not string them along as it is better for you to be honest about your true feelings than to lie about them to avoid hurting your partner's feelings. The truth is, either way they will be hurt, but it will hurt them even more if they learn that you did not respect them enough to be honest. Believe me, people will heal much quicker from being told the honest truth than they will from being fed a lie. In fact, they will respect you more despite the pain that they will initially feel.

In some cases, God allows us to get into relationships because of the valuable lessons that will be learned through the experience. Please know that God will not waste anything that you have experienced. It's just very important that you adhere to God's leading and instruction throughout so that you do not incur any blind spots or spiritual strongholds that will prohibit you from exiting if God shows you signs to do so. Overall, ignorance by way of taking a person and their goodness for granted is one reason why relationships fail.

Three Reasons Why Relationships Fail: # 2: Negligence

A nother component of why relationships fail is by way of a close cousin to ignorance called "negligence." Negligence in relationships can be explained by using this example of one partner in the relationship being taken for granted and no longer being seen in the light as being extraordinary. Due to time passing, their partner sees them as now being merely ordinary, redundant and not as exciting as they were once perceived when their relationship first began. Now, this is a sneaky component because it finds its way in even God ordained marriages and relationships simply because the individuals involved are not taking the time to maintain and feed their relationship.

If we take the time to maintain our vehicles by getting the oil changed, having the tires rotated, and maintaining the appearance by keeping it washed, what makes us think that our relationships should be treated differently if we want to have the best experience possible? Godly relationships are such a blessing to have and behold today. It is truly a luxury to see despite it being attainable to those who truly desire it and are willing to put forth the work.

In marriage and relationships that lead to marriage, I always inform those that I serve that we really *can* have fairytale marriages if we truly want them. The thing is, we *must* make the necessary investments in our relationships in order to have what we desire and having a fairytale marriage is not far-fetched in regard to living happily ever after. A fairy tale marriage does not mean that everything will be perfect, but it does mean that the pages of your story will reflect the details of you and your partner's ethical behaviors toward one another.

Depending on your ethics, this will lead to the outcome of how your story unfolds. If you've invested in things within your marriage that promote godliness, cohesivity, honesty, security, commitment, spontaneity, love and romance, fidelity, fun and respect, this is exactly what the love story of your marriage will be. Again, if this is what you mutually invest in and see as happily ever after, then happily is what you will be and ever after is the blessing! Just be sure to maintain it in order to avoid taking each other for granted.

Your marriage and relationship reflect "your" upkeep. Achieving an amazing marriage will require both individuals working to do 100% of their part in investing in the wellbeing of their union by inviting God into everything, attacking the issues and not each other, and being selfless and eager to serve each other out of honor, love, and respect for each other's needs and position. Incorporating healthy transparent communication in love is important as well as attending marital and premarital counseling to serve as maintenance or as a way to gain insight if marriage is the next step (for the unmarried).

I also encourage you to pray with and for each other and seal up every entry way known that the enemy may try to enter. Ways to seal up the entry ways that the enemy will attempt to invade include taking the stance to not entertain any ungodly advances or ungodly relationships of any sort. Remaining accountable and trustworthy by behaving as respectful in your significant other or spouse's "absence" as you would in their "presence" is also a must.

There are some other things that you can do to keep the fire lit. It's also important to complement each other, have regular date nights and worship together by attending the same church. Being each other's biggest fan as you're called to be each other's partner in purpose is crucial. Fight fair and never hit below the belt. Make love making (for those who are married) a priority to reestablish your bond and remain open to re-exploring each other's bodies with enthusiasm and incorporating spontaneity and healthy fun to keep the fire ablaze. It's also important to fellowship with other healthy couples and deliberately make every effort to express to your partner how much you choose them daily by gestures, affirmations, and however else God leads you.

Having a fairytale marriage does not equal perfection as

you will have disagreements and obstacles to address; however, by doing the things stated above, your fairy tale is very much attainable as you attack the issues together and show the enemy that your union is God sustained and destined to remain for our Heavenly Father's glory.

Three Reasons Why Relationships Fail: #3: It Is Self-Ordained Not God Ordained

A
nother component of why relationships fail is because the relationship was simply not God ordained but "self-ordained." In one too many cases due to various reasons, people tend to "forge" God's signature on a relationship and even a marriage that He never gave confirmation for them to enter into. This can occur when the parties involved either focus solely on chemistry, attractiveness, or feelings of anxiety in the form of FOMO (fear of missing out). In fact, it can also occur when we have many things in common and shared spiritual beliefs. Even with this, we can still not have God's permission to engage in a romantic relationship. Some people even find themselves believing that they have found their life partner due to shared trauma.

Some people believe that God does not tell us who we should or should not be with. I beg to differ in this thought.

When we are getting to know someone, it is imperative that we pray and ask God about who they are and what we are to do involving their presence in our lives based upon His instruction and cues. Please know that just because someone shows up in our life, we're attracted to them and have things in common does not mean that we necessarily have the green light to pursue a relationship with them.

The truth is that we can have chemistry and all of the things previously mentioned with a person and still not be the best for each other to build a life with. How might God give us confirmation you ask? Well, some ways that God will let us know that it's safe ground to pursue and move forward in a relationship is after praying, having a confirmed sense of unwavering peace with the person where the peace that you experience is not solely based upon the great or positively exciting situations that are presently going on around you. The peace that I'm speaking of is the unwavering peace that you *still* have with them when things are not ideal that confirms that even in the midst of frustrations or unpleasant circumstances, neither of you lose your sense of peace or security with each other and you do not have a fear of the other walking out due to the un-ideal situation that may be occurring.

Jesus states in John 14:27, "Peace I leave with you; my peace I give you. I do not give to you as the world gives. Do not let your hearts be troubled and do not be afraid." In other words, the peace that the world gives is circumstantial while the peace that Jesus gives us is sustained. This scripture fully encompasses the peace of God that I'm describing you will feel when I speak of the confirming peace that you should feel with your potential significant other. Additional confirmation after peace that God will give us about moving forward into marriage with our significant other is our sense of oneness with having the same faith, core values and morals along with similar interests in areas of great importance. If your experience with the person in which you're getting to know enlightens you in ways that make you better as a person, greater in your purpose and brings you closer to God and not further away from Him, then you're in good company. Having good, clear communication, respecting your mind and standards, and not encouraging you to compromise with them in order to gain their affection or keep their interest are signs as well.

The person that God will give you the green light to pursue and marry will also be consistent in their positive words and behavior towards you and those closest to you. This means that they will not say *or* do things to deliberately hurt you or those that you love as a way to gain control or get even if they do not get their way. The person that God will encourage you to pursue and marry will reflect His heart in various ways. Your partnership will enhance each other's lives causing each other to increase in strength and value as your strengths eliminate the limitations between you. Additionally, the person that God will encourage you to marry will know their purpose because God calls everything to bear fruit in its season of maturity which is synonymous to His perfect timing where we experience the best of what is to be offered and experienced.

Have you ever eaten a fruit that is not in season? If so, I'm sure you've noticed that the flavor of the fruit *in season* is *much* sweeter than the flavor experienced *out* of season. In fact, the flavor out of season may be bland, not as sweet or even sour which means that it is not at its best because it is being displayed out of its rightful season and timing. If you like, you can give this notion a try by tasting a fruit that is in season, and then try that same fruit when it is not in season. Take note of the difference in the taste and your enjoyment of that fruit.

Like fruit, anything and any relationship produced out of season will not provide the best experience. When your relationship is confirmed by God, you and your partner will be mature in mind and spirit and are willing to make healthy sacrifices for each other and make one another a priority as appropriate.

The person that God will confirm for you to marry will be genuinely affirming and show that they are trustworthy. They will have a committed spirit, have a great work ethic, are open to learning new things, have an active prayer life and have a teachable spirit amongst other things. Although these are a few things that God uses to allow you to know that it's safe ground to pursue a relationship that may eventually lead to marriage, the signs that God will give, or reveal are not limited to what I've mentioned. In the same breath, they should encompass what I have.

Certain issues can come into play when a couple does not have these above-mentioned green lights from God and decide to pursue marriage anyway in hopes that on the other side of saying, "I do," things will change for the better and that God will inevitably bless their union. Please hear me when I say that God is not obligated to bless what He did not ordain. Although He did create marriage, it does not mean that He ordained the marriage/ union that we set up and created just because we want Him to and were too anxious to either wait on His confirmation or didn't want to believe the red light that He presented because it did not line up with what *we* desired.

Does God have the capacity to intervene and out of His mercy assist a couple in fortifying their marriage despite them coming together and forging His signature? Yes. However, forging His signature on a union and then expecting Him to bless what He did not confirm is *"not"* what I recommend. In many cases He does not. Again, He is not obligated to support a union that He did not ordain. In addition, when we forge God's signature on what we want and do not include Him in the process for His perfect will to be revealed to us, it usually does not end well. In many cases both parties involved as well as those connected leave the marriage in an emotionally wounded state.

Divorce is equivalent to a death. The process of coming to this point is usually emotionally, spiritually, financially and mentally debilitating. Unfortunately, the individuals involved go through a grieving process and the only difference between grieving a marital death and the death of a loved one is that although the marriage is dead, the survivors of it are alive and must endure the pain of their once connected souls being forced to rip apart while still being alive.

The pain of this is experienced because of the spiritual bond being broken in lieu of the power of what marriage represents which is Christ's love for the church. Once this covenant is broken, those involved (if they're wise) must take the time needed to heal and allow God to repair them in the areas of their soul that only He can.

The blessing and mercy of God is that even when we have done things outside of His divine will for our lives that have caused us great pain, He is loving and merciful enough to take us back into His arms. He will repair our hearts and souls in such a way that when His work of healing is complete, we won't even look like the pain that we've experienced.

It is best to adhere to the green, yellow and red lights that God presents to us that signal whether we should move forward or not into a relationship or marriage. When we do, it will ensure that when we say, "I do," His provision will be attached to our vow as we stay connected to Him. It will save us from unnecessary heartache and grief and ensure that we will keep our peace. Prayer and obedience are key as it will keep us from experiencing the hardships that come with being in a relationship that is self-ordained, not God ordained.

Submission

S ubmission is a beautiful word in a healthy marriage; however, if you have an incorrect understanding of what it truly is, it's definitely a word tied to an action that you'll be resistant to surrender to. When a wife is loved correctly and a husband is respected as he should be, submission to one another is easy and quite frankly, it comes automatically. This is a characteristic of what makes holy matrimony holy. This is also another reason why a threefold cord is not easily broken (Ecclesiastes 4:12). So, what exactly is "submission," and how did some come to see or experience it as oppressive opposed to empowering and protective?

First and foremost, submission means to come up under a mission in support of and to support the goal or destination of the one in leadership. In biblical terms, since husbands and wives are to submit one to another, this means that the position as leader is subject to change depending on the circumstance or area of strength needed to fulfill their mission or goal. To break this down a little further from a biblical and spiritual standpoint, the word states to both husbands *and* wives in Ephesians 5:21-33 (NLT), "And further, submit one *to another* out of reverence for Christ.

For *wives*, this means submit to your husbands as to the Lord. For a husband is the head of *his* wife as Christ is the head of the church. He is the savior of his body, the church. As the church submits to Christ, so you wives should submit to your husbands in everything.

For *husbands,* this means "love" your wives, just as Christ loved the church. He gave up his life for her to make her holy and clean, washed by the cleansing of God's word. He did this to present her to himself as a glorious church without a spot or wrinkle or any other blemish. Instead, she will be holy and without fault.

In the same way, husbands ought to love their wives as they love their own bodies. For a man who loves his wife shows love for himself. No one hates his own body but feeds and cares for it, just as Christ cares for the church. And we are members of his body. As the scriptures say, "A man leaves his father and mother and is joined to his wife, and the two are united into one. This is a great mystery, but it is an illustration of the way Christ, and the church are one. So again, I say, each man must love his wife as he loves himself, and the wife must respect her husband."

As we begin to further interpret this scripture to assess the reason why the word "submission" (for some) has taken on a negative connotation, I've found that it is because one too many spiritually immature individuals have taken the word and act of "submission" and either perverted it or misused it for their own fleshly desires to dominate. The need to dominate for the individual that has perverted or misused the sanctity of submission can more than likely be a result of either their own insecurities, an unhealthy upbringing, a direct reflection of being under unhealthy spiritual leadership that teaches submission incorrectly or all the above.

Either way, these variables deserve attention and if not properly addressed, an unhealthy perception of what it means to submit will continue and God's design for it will be further misinterpreted. Unfortunately, if it continues unaddressed, one too many wives will fall under the hands of unjust treatment, and one too many husbands will be led by misinformation and unhealthy spiritual leadership that teaches them to oppress their partners. This is not God's way or His will.

Submission in marriage with the man being the head signifies his authority in leadership with being responsible for covering, loving, providing for and protecting his wife as he leads her through life as he submits to Christ who leads him. It should also be mentioned in general that studying the Word of God should not be limited to what your Pastor or Bishop preaches or teaches on a Sunday morning or evening bible study. I am a firm believer that studying the word of God should also take place at home on your own. This way no one will be able to lead you astray as you're also reading the word for yourself and making your own interpretations with the guidance of the Holy spirit, a concordance, or new living translation bible that helps to further reveal scripture in context.

Getting back to submission with the focus on the wife submitting to her husband, as we look at Ephesians 5:21-33, there is not one word or line that suggests that submission requires her to not have an opinion. There is also not one line that implies that she is to leave her brain on the bed and move through life as if submitting requires one to lose their sense of value, thought or purpose. I have heard of *some* men *and* women viewing submission or the act of submitting as a position where the wife is subservient to her husband. This flawed connotation that her "submitting" entails him making "all" of the major decisions is absurd. Just to be clear, I do understand and respect the fact that as Christ is the head of man, that man is the head of the woman due to the position of divine order, leadership, covering and protection.

The issue that I've seen is that some husbands have used

this scripture to dictate and diminish their wives and render her opinion and position as the neck (since the neck supports the head) as not as valuable in comparison to his. Many are misled due to this thinking in which they further misinterpret the scripture and use it out of context as mentioned before, to dominate. This contrary and ungodly belief engineered to dominate God's daughters could not be further from the heart, truth and will of our loving God in Ephesians 5:22-33.

If a wife submitting to her husband means that she should not have a voice or have any input in decisions being made for their household and the mission at hand that she is called to support, then there would be no reason for it to be stated in God's own words in Genesis 2:18 NLT that, it is not good for the man to be alone. I will make a "helper" who is just right for him. It can be further mentioned that if a wife is supposed to have no opinion or major significance in her husband's life then there would be no need for the word of God to state in Proverbs 18:22, He who finds a wife finds a good thing and obtains *favor* from the Lord.

The correct position for both the husband and wife to take is just as the word states, for them to submit one to another. They were created for each other, and it pleases God for a husband and wife to be on one accord with the husband loving his wife as Christ loves the church and the wife respecting her husband as the head and her covering (protector) as he submits to God. As she submits to him and he submits to her, together they exemplify God's divine order as they both submit unto Him. To submit by God's standards is to honor and there is no oppression in honor - only love and respect. Submission by God's standard in marriage is a beautiful thing when you understand its true context!

For those who question what to do when a husband and wife do not agree on what should be done, the answer is to follow the direction of peace, focus on what you do agree upon, take inventory of *who's stronger* in the subject area of your situation and let those variables along with the Holy Spirit lead you to make the best decision.

Although the husband is responsible for ultimately covering, protecting and leading the family in Christ, *wisdom* is the principal thing. It has nothing to do with gender but everything to do with order and what moves the mission in God's divine direction. If the best idea for the family happens to come from the wife who God made as her husband's helper (which does not exclude the husband as being an aid), then that's the decision that should be made. After all, since the two are united as one, no matter who has the better idea for the decision, God gets the glory because His idea of submission prevails and the family wins.

Lagniappe Note: Love, honor and respect go hand in hand and cannot be separated. There is *no* gray area between them. Unfortunately, what I've continued to observe is a great divide. On one side, I see one too many people disrespect who they "claim" to love. On the other side, I see how others show love and honor to whom they respect. This leads me to say that where there is a lack of respect, there is definitely an absence of love and honor in its truest God-sense and meaning.

When people respect you, this is when they truly show you that they love you in the form of honor. To respect someone is to honor them, which is the depth of what love is truly about. When a person respects you, they dare not intentionally behave out of order towards you because out of their love for you, they honor you. When a person deliberately disrespects or dishonors you (this goes both ways), it is a direct reflection of their immaturity and lack of respect, honor and true love for you. For those in waiting, God's best in His perfect timing will reflect love, honor, and respect. Nothing less. Although people are under construction and do make mistakes, when true love, honor and respect for their significant other or spouse is at the core of a person's heart, the evidence will be shown through earnest repentance of their ungodly actions. This is followed by changed behavior that reflects love, honor and respect towards their partner which confirms their repentance. This confirmation makes room for reconciliation (if at all possible) and moves forward to bring God glory.

Married with Children

Spouses come before children and there's a godly order to this thing called being married with children. Unfortunately, so many either overlook the order or have never seen it done, which is why they never operate in it. On so many occasions I have witnessed couples become so engrossed in their roles as parents that they forsake the blessing and privilege of being lovers and catering to their spouse and marital union. Unfortunately, by the time their children grow up and graduate from high school and leave for college, the couple that neglected to nurture their union to focus on parenting no longer know who each other is.

Despite being under the same roof for countless years, what I've seen more often are the remnants of two lovers who lost each other over time. In some cases, the marriage can be revived, but in other cases, I've seen that it was beyond repair. As the time passed, both individuals changed without taking notice and or the spouse that expressed the need for attention and affection that got constantly ignored learned how to either live without their spouse's attention, lost their desire for them, or sought their need for attention to be fulfilled elsewhere. Please know that I am in no way condoning or excusing infidelity; however, I would be remiss if I didn't mention it as a factor within some marriages when one spouse feels neglected and their requests for attention go unanswered.

It can also be mentioned that in the midst of it all, parenting is work and it is truly another level of sacrifice. Although parenting requires sacrifice, parents should never have to sacrifice the life of their marriage to care for the children that their love created. For husbands, if your wife expresses that she is exhausted when you express your desire for sexual intimacy, please do your due diligence to help her around the home so that she can not only have the desire to be intimate, but have the energy needed to do so amongst other things.

I have had the opportunity to see the dynamics of marriages from multiple angles while being a therapist. Because of this, I have also seen the controversy. For example, some husbands feel that since they work and provide for their family financially that when they come home, they should not have to do or be expected to do anything but relax. Meanwhile, their wife who may also work outside of the home is not given the liberty to check out and relax when she gets home because upon her arrival, (that is if she did not already have carpool duty), she must immediately switch modes and be a mother, cook, nurse, counselor, teacher, and homework checker. This is the case if her spouse does not assist. By the time all of this is over, and the kids are finally in bed, her husband expects her to turn into his lover in which the next day (if he's not a hands-on dad), the wife must turn around and do this all over again.

Husbands, if this is how your household looks, *please* pay close attention to the words that I am about to say because I am trying to help you save your marriage and also help you and your wife to rekindle or maintain a healthy sex life. **If you want your**

wife to have the capacity to be as exciting "post children" as she was "pre children," she is going to need your help because the tables have turned. Life is different with children.

Remember, they are *also* competing for her attention. Your wife needing your help means assisting her daily with either bathing the kids, helping them with homework, sweeping around the house and vacuuming, washing the dishes, cooking, heating up the food or ordering takeout for family dinner if needed. As you do this, when she gets home with the kids, it's less for her to do which makes more time for you two to connect. Anything that will help her to have more done in less time will be a great help.

In the end, stepping up will not only allow you to see all that she has to do on top of working outside of the home, but it will also help her to have some energy for herself. It will allow you both to have more alone time, energy, and be able to engage in sexual intimacy at the end of the night if you both choose. When your wife see's the effort that you're putting forth to help her with the responsibilities of caring for your children and maintaining the home that you've both created and built, believe me, she will have more desire for you because women have a great tendency to respond sexually when they are shown how much they are appreciated and supported. At the end of each day, you both walk away winning and both individuals close the day feeling heard, appreciated, loved, and respected.

Having some much-needed time to discuss ways that you can prioritize your marriage is important because it reminds you that you are lovers first and parents second. Not all marriages are the same and gender roles are interchangeable. For those who have spouses that are stay at home moms and dads or if you're reading this and you happen to be one, the information mentioned above about needing assistance from your spouse is for you as well. At the end of the day, no matter your position, teamwork makes the dreamwork! Your marriages are worth it. In the end, your children will love you for not neglecting each other since keeping your marriage a priority in addition to nurturing them is what helped to keep their home united.

Lagniappe Note: Parents, please remember that your young children will grow up and leave you to start their own lives and families. When that time comes, if not appropriately addressed, you will find yourself left with a spouse that you no longer know and vice versa. It is important to make children a priority, but it should not be at the expense of losing your marriage. Balance is key and God will help you to find the balance that you need. Just invite Him in through prayer and allow the Holy Spirit to lead. Your children will thank you. I know I thank mine for their example and God gets the glory!!!

Things that you can do to prioritize your marriage are:

1. **Pray together.** Prayer is a wonderful form of intimacy that is like oxygen and armor to a union that one too many couples overlook. When you engage in prayer together, it is a time where you consciously solicit the presence of God. It is in prayer that you'll both gain supernatural insight and strengthen your union

as you reinforce your threefold cord with God. It is not easily broken.

2.Go on a day date. One example is using that PTO to take a day off from work, drop the kids off at daycare or school, and get breakfast at a local spot that you've always wanted to try. After that you can catch a matinee. You'll have much of the day to yourself to do whatever you and your honey would like...uninterrupted! And if your kids have aftercare?!! Let your imagination flow!

3. $5 Tuesday at the movies and then Chick- Fil-A (Take it back to the teenage years of dating on a budget).

4. Walk in the park or have a picnic at home or in your yard. Make it fun!

5. Role play. Dance at home. Any form of intimacy and time alone to bond is important. It's *not* always about spending a lot of money. There's a time and place for it and "*always*" is not.

6. **Try new restaurants and be a tourist in your own city**. You would be surprised at what you don't know about your city or town, and you can make another memory by learning together.

7. **Walk down memory lane.** Go back to the place you first met (if possible) and talk about *then* versus *now* and the BLESSINGS of your now. Even if you can't go back to the physical spot, you can still talk about it and revisit the emotions that you felt. Conversation is key!

8. **Cook dinner and make dessert together at home without the kids.** If a family member can't watch the kids, do your due diligence and find a reputable drop-in center. Since the kids won't be around, make "each other" your appetizer, enjoy your meal and then follow up again with making "each other" your dessert... all over the house, and get innovative!

9. **Go to a concert or comedy show**. It's all about being together, growing together and making memories. Since we're currently

in a pandemic and you may feel uncomfortable with going into public places, if possible, go virtually!

10. **Go to marriage retreats.** Marital maintenance is key and engaging in enriching activities and gaining information on how to continuously fortify your marriage with other married couples is priceless.

11. **Take vacations away and do multiple staycations.** Go to a nice hotel for the weekend or in the middle of the week. Be spontaneous!

12. **Take a road trip to a place that you've always wanted to go.** Opt for a place that's not too far but not too close if driving far is not your forte!

13. **Make love- making fun and do it often!** Don't stick to the routine. Play sex games and read books to gain insight on how to keep it lively! Remember, the marital bed is undefiled (Hebrews 13:4) and you're both evolving mentally, emotionally, spiritually

and sexually.

14. **Take time to check in to assess each other's desires and needs and do so with an open, nonjudgmental mind.** Once your spouse expresses his or her need, be quick to adhere to it unless for some reason it makes you uncomfortable. If this is the case, talk about it with your spouse. See how you may both be able to meet in the middle where you both are comfortable with the outcome and feel acknowledged and respected.

15. **Maintain a regular date night and dress up!** Just like you make work a priority, you should make date night a priority as well!

16. **Do something that you've never done before but would like to do. Be sure** to do it together! One way to make this easy is to write events on a strip of paper that are feasible now as well as later. Fold the stripes of paper up and put them in a jar or container. Each week you can pull from the container and that will be your date destination. If it's something that isn't currently

feasible, make plans to do it by looking at your calendars and set a date for when it can be done, stick with the date and save up for it. Because you're still going out, pick another event from the container and get ready! Again, memories are everything so have fun with my suggestions. Create some of your own or add a spin on them to make it uniquely you!

Sex

Sex is God's celebratory gift to a husband and wife in Holy matrimony. It is so powerful and beautiful that it can only be adequately contained in the covenant of Holy matrimony. As we begin to talk more about sex, I feel that it is important to express what sex is from a godly perspective to set the bar high which is where it started and in the eyes of God, where it will always be. In today's society, we can all honestly say that the world has downplayed sex as something casual. Its sacredness and purity have not been valued as they should be. The world or worldly thinking calls God's way of addressing sex as "old fashioned" and "outdatedAshaving it outside of the confines of marriage, we now have more children being born into single parent homes (which was not God's original design for the family). We have sexually transmitted diseases that can either harm or take the life of a person which goes totally against God's origin for sex as being celebratory and life giving. We now deal with the issue of sexual addiction - addictions to pornography and multiple sexual partners. Unsatiable sexual appetites and the inability to be emotionally intimate with one another in romantic relationships is present also.

Sex outside of marriage has caused many to have "unhealthy" spiritual soul ties that cause an individual to be unable to truly experience mental, emotional and spiritual peace within themselves. It prohibits them from having a healthy connection within their marriage due to not spiritually divorcing themselves from past sexual experiences and in turn place them upon their spouse. For those of you who are not yet married but have had sexual experiences in previous relationships, it would behoove you to do your due diligence in divorcing your mind and spirit from those experiences. If you do not, it will definitely pose an issue for you in your marriage due to the weight of sexual comparison and your propensity to still be emotionally and spiritually connected to those of your past experiences. Believe me, if you do not spiritually purge yourself from your past sexual experiences with the help of God, they will be sure to make themselves present when you say, "I do." Remember, the adversary does not want your marriage to survive; therefore, he will go back into your history and try to see if he can revive what you thought was dead if you haven't severed those ties.

Methods that you can take to sever those unhealthy soul ties are to make sure that objects that were given to you by a previous partner are discarded. This includes all pictures, clothes, or items that remind you of them. It's also important that you deliberately fast and pray to invite God into those places in your spirit to remove all emotional and spiritual attachments to them. The reason why it is important to get rid of physical items is because of the spiritual connection that they carry which keep you attached.

For those that have children with a previous sex partner which causes them to still connect with their ex, it is totally understood that you cannot divorce yourself from your children. You can still follow the above suggestions within reason. For parents who have children that express their desire to have individual or family portraits that include their biological parent, your kids do have that right to that desire because it represents their parent and family of origin. It can be placed in their bedroom.

It is still important that you do the necessary work that is needed to purify your soul. This could also include therapy so that you do not find yourself triggered by seeing the picture. Some may feel that it is unnecessary to discard items from your past relationships and on one end, I can understand their thinking. The thing is, if when you see the item, it reminds you of your previous relationship and memories (good or bad) come flooding back, it needs to go. If not and it sincerely causes no nostalgia or flashbacks, then I understand your reason for keeping it; nonetheless, use wise discretion.

Another issue that I feel needs to be addressed on the topic of sex in marriage is frequency. The demands of life and work put pressure on our lives. It is important to not allow the demands of life to put a wedge between you and your spouse about sexual intimacy. For those who are married and do not have the responsibility of raising kids, sex may be much easier for you to have spontaneously. For those who are married with kids, it may not be as easy. Although it may not be, just as you make plans to attend special events or take your kids to practice by putting the event on your calendar, you can do the same for sex as it should also be a priority.

Remember, sex is a gift that God has given to those who are married so please do not overlook this blessing. This is an area that the adversary will target to cause division if you do. It's also important to talk about sexual desires and expectations along with the frequency of it before you get married so that going in you already understand what's expected and desired. If while discussing sex you find that there's an area that your partner expressed desire for that poses as a discomfort for you, it is important that you share that information with them and discuss how you can possibly meet in the middle. If not, discuss the reasons why. Please note that it is always important for you both to be on the same page when it comes to intimacy, your needs, and desires. The only way that you can get there is by having healthy discussions about it. No one is a mind reader.

Regarding singles, I have spoken with some who have expressed that they have either avoided talking about sex in their relationship because they are unsure if they should discuss it to avoid triggers (since they were actively practicing abstinence). I have spoken to others who thought that it would be inappropriate to discuss it since they were in ministry. I am here to tell you that it would behoove you to talk about sex, your desires, and expectations so that you can know if you are on the same page about it or not.

Sex is a natural concept of life so let's not make it taboo because guess what, people are doing it every day. Besides that, you can talk about sex in a respectful way without being offensive. Furthermore, having healthy conversations about sex will reveal your significant other's comfort level or lack thereof. It also sets the platform for you both to have greater insight about the other to discuss your differences and similarities and discover if sex is an area of past trauma that you can address together.

Another thing to keep in mind is that sex in marriage should not be withheld as punishment but neither should it be forced or demanded. Truth be told, in marriage, love making and the desire to do so should be the fruit or response that naturally evolves from seeds of love and honor planted in the soil of the receiver's mind and heart. These seeds should be planted mutually and consistently. Being a person's husband or wife never gives either spouse the right to sexually force themselves upon the other should one or the other not desire to engage. If this happens, this is rape, it is illegal and yes, it goes both ways, husband to wife and wife to husband. Withholding sex as punishment for your spouse is a recipe for disaster. It can come across as manipulative, controlling and selfish depending on the issue. It is also important for a spouse to not deliberately do something that they know upsets their spouse, and then want sex after. It can come across as selfish, manipulative, unloving, disrespectful, arrogant and inconsiderate which can turn into full on emotional and mental abuse if it continues unchecked.

When you have disagreements, it is important to try your very best to get back on the same page. Discuss the issue to resolve it, but never use sex as a manipulative tactic or way to get what you want. Do not withhold sex because you did not get what you want. If an issue arises that has caused you to be legitimately upset and emotionally unavailable now due to the need to process your thoughts, not wanting to be touched is understandable. I encourage you to always seek the quickest route to peace where you can both talk and walk away from the conversation feeling respected, heard, honored, and seal your reconciliation with lovemaking opposed to walking away angry and dishonored. Pray about everything and lean not on your own understanding.

You can't make REAL love until you're willing to become completely naked. Many are fine with just getting physically naked in order to have sex, but when having sex without being emotionally naked (as in vulnerable or open), those involved are just having emotionless sex. **It comes off as movements with no meaning where the agenda is to reach orgasm without intimate connection.**

On the contrary, allowing yourself to become emotionally naked with your spouse and vice versa provides a place within your relationship where you're both completely safe in your vulnerability. This is when you truly experience God's intent of what making love is in the form of deep intimacy which is synonymous to the depth of worship. The beauty of love making in marriage is that this love making reaches higher levels of intimacy and connectedness as it's endorsed by the Creator and allows both husband and wife to know that even Heaven backs up their union and acts of uniting as one.

Afterword

As this book comes to a close, my prayer is that you have been spiritually, mentally and emotionally enlightened and that the information that you have received through reading my book gives you hope, valuable information and a platform to excel in giving, receiving and navigating healthy, godly love. I hope that it will richly bless your life and leave a lasting legacy. Whether you're in the amazing season of singleness or marriage in motion, God's intent is for you to go from glory to glory and achieve His picture of holiness in your seasons. May you be whole, richly blessed and live in the truth of God's word that states that when God blesses a thing, He makes it rich and adds no sorrow to it. Congratulations and blessings in advance!!!

Oh, and one last **Lagniappe note -** No matter what you have or have *not* seen, what you need will be present because there is no shortage in God! He'll even make what you need up if He has to! The thing is, He doesn't have to because it's already done!!

That's just the kind of God that we serve as He'll do exceedingly, abundantly and above all that we could ever ask or think according to the power that works in us (Ephesians 3:20). That power is the power of Jesus Christ. With this, we can never go wrong!!

Acknowledgements

To be honest, there are so many people that I would like to thank as my ability to write this book has come from God, my convictions, my parents, my prayer partners, my Spiritual fathers, the people that I seek to empower, as well as my Kingdom husband, the man of God that I have yet to meet yet know exists.

Thank you, God, for giving me the courage and the strength through the Holy Spirit to live my truth and go against the grain of mainstream society to live a life completely sold out for you! God, you alone through my Savior and Lord Jesus Christ have sustained me on the inside when all other things and people faded away. I thank God for my hope and my trust in knowing that as I seek His face, trust in His divine timing, and allow the Holy spirit to lead me that I will always win and receive what is in God's hands, especially for me.

I thank God for my parents that were my first example of

peace and harmony in a godly marriage. Mama, I saw the work and dedication that both you and daddy put in to make sure that Emily and I had a healthy and sound upbringing where God was the covering and center of our home in love. I am forever grateful for the example that you both showed me on how to choose and what to accept when it comes to marriage. I know that marriage takes work, and I witnessed the opposition that you and daddy faced to keep your marriage secure, yet in the midst of seeing what you faced, I watched you both prevail for God's glory.

I thank my prayer partners that include my mom Denise, my sister Emily, and my sisters in Christ Wanda Compton, Apostle Tiffany Joseph, Jeanean Sanders and many others for covering me in prayer as I have walked the straight and narrow.

I would also like to thank Bishop Samuel R. Blakes and Bishop Robert (R.C) Blakes Jr. for preaching and teaching the Word of God and helping me to grow spiritually after the passing of my earthly father. God knew that I needed multiple words from two strong men of God to help restore my heart and strength. He chose you two and I'm grateful. I also thank the many people that have given me the opportunity to serve them in both their season of singleness and in marriage as you could have all chosen someone else, but God saw it fit that we would cross paths and He would get the glory from our working history.

Last but certainly not least, I must thank my dear future husband. My love, if you could only know how much I love and respect you without having met you. It may sound strange, but I know you in spirit and have felt you on various occasions because you feel like home. Home is a place where I have always been safe. I honestly have places within myself and locations on reserve in my heart and spirit that no one has ever entered or experienced because I've saved those sacred places for you and only you. I have a very strong feeling that we will be meeting soon and if you happen to read this book after we have, just know that I've always been excited to meet you, which is the reason why I took the time to prepare myself for you. The best part is, we have

the rest of our lives to focus so much on living that we never

think of departing.

Index

A

B

C

D

F

H

I

voice of God, 21

W

waiting, 16, 24, 26, 31, 34, 38, 40, 58, 175

About the Author

Robin Webster MS, LPC, NCC is a native of New Orleans, LA. She is an ordained minister and the CEO and Owner of her private practice, "Tower of Refuge Christian Counseling, LLC. " Robin is a bilingual (English and Spanish speaking) licensed professional counselor, nationally certified counselor, author and motivational speaker.

After earning her Bachelor of Arts degree with honors in Psychology in Spring 2005 from Southern University at New Orleans, Robin attended Minnesota State University at Mankato (MSU) in Fall 2005 and majored in (CSP) Professional Community Counseling with a Focus in Marriage and Family Therapy. Upon graduating from MSU with her Master of Science degree in Spring 2007 and becoming nationally certified to counsel with the National Board of Certified Counselors, Robin began working in the counseling field and later became independently licensed to counsel with the Louisiana Professional

Counselors Board of Examiners in June of 2012.

Throughout Robin's 15 years of service in the therapeutic field, Robin has worked with expecting and parenting teens, as a Crisis Counselor, and Suicide Prevention and Intervention Specialist. She has worked with diverse clientele that includes teens and adolescents, adults, couples and families dealing with hardships, along with survivors of both domestic violence, sexual abuse and other trauma. Robin has also served in assisting individuals living with mental health disorders, grief and loss, terminal illnesses and impaired self-esteem by assisting them in building and rediscovering the joys of hope and new reasons to embrace each day with strength and confidence.

Robin considers it an honor to serve and has loved serving since childhood. As a result of this and believing in God's mission of love and witnessing the restorative power of Jesus Christ, her efforts and dedication to her life's calling of Christian counseling have increased. When deciding to open her private practice, Robin did so through the leading of the Holy Spirit, the love of her Christian faith and seeing the great need for faith and therapy to beautifully collide in order to serve the "whole person" which entails the mind, body, soul and spirit.

Robin is active in participating in Intercessory prayer and is involved with Iron Sharpens Iron Ministry where she and other clergy, brothers and sisters in Christ pray together every Tuesday on the behalf of each other and others in need. Robin also led the Singles Ministry at New Home Ministries for 6 and a half years until God transitioned her to rest and spiritually prepare for an additional position in ministry.

Ms. Webster is a member of Alpha Kappa Alpha Sorority, Inc. Because Robin loves healthy godly marriages and relationships and understands that not everyone will attend therapy, she figured that another way to assist them in healing and gaining greater insight into building a blessed legacy in marriage could be found in the pages of this book that God inspired her to write. Ultimately, Robin believes that in her life, the only things that will last are the things that she does for Christ, and she finds joy in assisting others in living their best God ordained life.

Made in the USA
Columbia, SC
25 August 2022

65413540R00117